HENRY HOWARD
EARL OF SURREY

Henry Howard
EARL OF SURREY

Selected Poems

*Edited with an Introduction
and Notes by*
DENNIS KEENE

FyfieldBooks

First published in Great Britain 1985
by the Carcanet Press
208 Corn Exchange Building
Manchester M4 3BQ

British Library Cataloguing in Publication Data

Surrey, Henry Howard, *Earl of*
  Selected poems.
  I. Title   II. Keene, Dennis
  821'.2   PR2370.A1

ISBN 0-85635-552-6

The Publisher acknowledges financial assistance
from the Arts Council of Great Britain

Typeset by Bryan Williamson, Swinton, Berwickshire
Printed in Great Britain by SRP Ltd, Exeter

Contents

— Meditations
+ Morality/Biblical

LAST POEMS

Introduction

SURREY and Wyatt have been linked together since their appearance in Tottel's *Miscellany* (1557) and, until this century, Surrey's poetry had been the more highly valued of the two. The revolution in taste which brought the metaphysical poets into fashion reversed this judgment so conclusively that nowadays there are three different editions of Wyatt's complete poems in print, but not one of Surrey. In fact the last complete edition came out in 1920. Surrey, it would seem, no longer matters, and even those people who might have been expected to have a good word for him are unenthusiastic. C.S. Lewis's final judgment is that 'by any sane standard, however, he is merely a man who served his generation well and has left one or two poems of paramount, though moderate value;' and his most recent editor (twenty years ago, that is), Emrys Jones, concludes that 'although he created a distinct literary personality, a severe criticism will find his achievement small in scale and flawed.'

One appreciates the tact of that 'severe criticism', but Jones does not suggest such severity is misplaced. If one adds to this faint praise the dismissals by Yvor Winters and others, or an edition of Surrey's *Aeneid* in which the editor's main concern is to track down borrowings from Gavin Douglas (even *italicizing* the text where this nebulous process is supposed to have taken place — editorial impertinence of a high order indeed), then Surrey appears as a poet already consigned to a proper oblivion, henceforth to exist only as the subject of an academic article or reluctant Ph. D. every few years. The more tolerant attitude taken towards Surrey in specialist journals over the past two decades is little more than a natural reaction to previous excesses, and represents no real change in overall taste.

Yet Wyatt was never valued above Surrey until this century. The book we know as Tottel's *Miscellany* was originally entitled *Songs and sonnets, written by the right honourable Lord Henry Howard late Earl of Surrey, and other*; 'other' being Wyatt *et al.* When Sidney spoke of the English poets he named Chaucer, Sackville, Surrey and Spenser, but made no mention of Wyatt. It would be wrong to make too much of this, for the predominance given Surrey by Tottel was a social rather than a critical act in acknowledgement of Surrey's superior rank, and Sidney's remarks on Surrey are so brief ('and in the Earl of Surrey's lyrics many things tasting of a noble mind') that it seems it was the image of Surrey as the dashing soldier-poet cut down in his prime which really interested him, as it also fascinated creators of romanticized fiction like Nashe and Drayton. Puttenham, who saw Wyatt and Surrey as 'the first reformers of our English metre and style' (*The Art of English Poesie*, 1589) claimed to have found 'little difference' between them, but this was probably because they were equally useful in providing rhetorical tropes for his inspection. By Puttenham's time, in fact, both were museum pieces, and yet during the two decades of real influence, the 1560s and 1570s, Surrey was the dominant figure, because he was seen as having achieved a revolution in the rhythm and vocabulary of poetry which Wyatt had merely commenced. One can say it was Surrey who determined the nature of poetic vocabulary for the following two hundred years.

Despite this real and lasting influence, interest in both Surrey and Wyatt soon waned, and may have even disappeared entirely during the seventeenth century. Since Surrey provides the first instance of narrative blank verse in our history, it is surprising that Milton seems to have shown no awareness of his example, going instead to the Italian models which Surrey had earlier absorbed. It was not until the eighteenth century that attention was paid to him again, as the sixteenth-century poet who had attempted the same neo-classical reform of English verse as that carried out by Waller and Denham in the seventeenth. Pope certainly read Surrey with interest, but the profundity of that interest is doubtful, his main attention being on the romantic image created by Nashe in *The Unfortunate*

Traveller.

> Here noble Surrey felt the sacred Rage,
> *Surrey*, the *Granville* of a former age:
> Matchless his pen, victorious was his lance;
> Bold in the lists, and graceful in the Dance:
> In the same Shades the Cupids tun'd his lyre,
> To the same Notes, of love, and soft Desire:
> Fair *Geraldine*, bright Object of his Vow,
> Then fill'd the Groves, as heav'nly Myra now.

(*Windsor Forest*, 291-8: George Granville, Lord Lansdowne, to whom the poem is dedicated, had already been praised by Pope for his 'moving lays'; understandably, since Granville was an up and coming politician. History, however, in the shape of Dr Johnson, was to deliver a different verdict on his poetry — 'trifles written by idleness and published by vanity' — and only two years later his political career came to an abrupt end with the accession of George the First).

Although it would be unwise to make much of such obsequiousness, these lines indicate some kind of high and settled reputation for Surrey, which persisted through the eighteenth century, culminating in the magnificent Nott edition of 1815; from which point onwards it enters into a gradual decline. Presumably it was the terms in which the eighteenth century praised him which led to this decline, since he was seen as the champion of neo-classical poetic virtues, the 'smooth numbers', 'unconceited intelligibility' and 'elegance of sentiment' for which Thomas Warton had admired him in 1781. Before considering that decline, however, it will be as well to give some account of the life which Warton justly saw as throwing 'so much light on the character and subjects of his poetry'.

Henry Howard was born early in 1517, eldest son of Thomas Howard, Earl of Surrey, who became the third Duke of Norfolk in 1524, and will henceforth be referred to as Norfolk. On the death of his first wife in 1512, Norfolk married Elizabeth Stafford, a great heiress, daughter of the Duke of Buckingham. The Howard family had already attained eminence through a marriage to a descendant of Edward I, and had the right to bear the royal arms in their escutcheon. This closeness to the throne was to be the main cause of Surrey's death in his thirtieth year, as it had also been for his grandfather, the Duke of Buckingham, in 1521.

Surrey spent his childhood in the country, although rarely in one place for long. As heir to the greatest land-owner in England he had a privileged upbringing in houses where scholars and poets were frequent guests; but relations between his parents were unhappy, Norfolk taking a mistress from among his own household in 1526, and they separated eventually in 1534. Norfolk was often away from home, so the mother had charge of Surrey's upbringing. Little is known of this, but it is a fact that both Surrey and his sister, Mary, supported their father in his various quarrels with their mother.

In 1530, aged thirteen, Surrey joined the Duke of Richmond at Windsor, where he was educated with him for the next two years (see note to poem 17). Richmond, Henry Fitzroy (b. 1519), was the bastard son of Henry VIII by Elizabeth Blount, and thought of as his heir. Henry VIII had a high opinion of Surrey, who was already famous for his beauty and wit, and during the political intrigues which surrounded Wolsey's downfall in 1529 it was suggested that Surrey might marry Princess Mary, Henry's only legitimate child. In 1532 he was, however, contracted in marriage to Lady Frances de Vere, daughter of the Earl of Oxford. She was a year younger than Surrey and they did not actually live together as man and wife until 1535. In October 1532 he accompanied Henry VIII and Anne Boleyn (Surrey's cousin) to France (Wyatt was one of the attendant courtiers on this occasion), and he remained there with Richmond as security for the treaty signed between the two kings. Surrey's stay of a year at the French court gave him some idea of the esteem in which poetry was held on the Continent, and probably actual acquaintance with Italian poets who visited the court. In 1553 Anne Boleyn's coronation took place, establishing the Howards as the most influential family in the land. This influence was confirmed by the marriage of Surrey's sister Mary to Richmond in September, although the two young men continued their bachelor life at Windsor (having returned in August).

Surrey's eldest son was born in 1536, and one assumes he had been living with his wife since 1535. The Earl of Surrey was a courtesy title, so financially he was totally dependent on his father, and a begging letter written in 1535 suggests that the young married couple's allowance was not all that generous. They were living at Norfolk's principal residence of Kenninghall and did not have their own home for some years. On 22 July 1536 the Duke of Richmond (who never lived with his Howard wife) died. The fortunes of the Howards had suddenly declined, for in May of that same year Anne Boleyn had been tried and condemned for adultery. The Seymours were raised to power with Sir Edward Seymour created Viscount Beauchamp, and Jane Seymour, his sister, made queen; a power they were to retain until her death in October 1537.

In 1537 Surrey was imprisoned for striking Sir Edward Seymour (see note to poem 17). Little is recorded for 1538 except the birth of his second son. He was living a retired life in the country and it is a fair assumption that he wrote a good deal of poetry at this time. In 1539 he was busy with building sea defences in Norfolk. On May Day, 1540, he acquitted himself with great honour at the grand tournament for Anne of Cleves, whom Henry VIII had married in January of that year. Surrey had a particularly violent clash with Viscount Lisle (John Dudley, one of the 'new men', like Seymour, whom Surrey so despised) but the king was apparently delighted by this display of valour. One comment made on Surrey this year was that 'It is the most foolish proud boy that is in England.'

The fall of Thomas Cromwell, followed by Henry VIII's marriage to Catherine Howard, Surrey's seventeen-year-old cousin, put the Howards back in power. In May 1541 Surrey received the Order of the Garter, and the Stewardship of Cambridge University in the same year. Catherine's execution for adultery in February 1542 did the Howards little good, but was not as disastrous for Norfolk and Surrey as might have been expected, probably because their military talents were in demand that year. Surrey was, however, imprisoned for a short while (see note to poem 24), took part in an expedition against the Scots, was imprisoned again in 1543 (see note to poem 28), and then spent that summer in the country, probably another period of poetic activity. In October he joined the English troops at the siege of Landrecy.

1544 was occupied with the building of Surrey House (see note to poem 37), and later in the year he was made Marshal of the Field in France and put in charge of the siege at Montreuil. His heroic attempt to take the town (see note to poem 36) failed, and he spent the winter in Boulogne, which was now besieged by the French. He led a bold excursion against them in January 1545. After returning to England to raise an army of 5,000 Norfolk veterans, he was appointed Commander at Boulogne in September, and given the title of Lieutenant General of the King on Sea and Land. This was the high point of his military career, although his encouragement of Henry VIII to continue this pointless war made him unpopular with the Privy Council, who were embarrassed by the expense of holding Boulogne and wished to come to terms with the French.

A military setback in January 1546, in which some gentlemen of rank were killed, completed the annoyance of the Privy Council, for Surrey was well known for his willingness to risk the lives of himself and his officers. He was recalled to England on March 21, but it does not appear that he had yet incurred the king's displeasure to any serious extent. A peace treaty signed on June 7 returned Boulogne to the French. At about the same time Norfolk took up once more his old plan (see note to poem 23) to create an alliance between the Howards and the Seymours by marrying the Duchess of Richmond

12

(Surrey's sister) to Sir Thomas Seymour, and three Howard children (including Surrey's two sons) to three of those of the Earl of Hertford (i.e., Sir Edward Seymour, Surrey's great rival). The plan received the royal blessing, but Surrey, who had not been consulted and only learned of the plan by hearsay, violently objected to any alliance with the worst of the 'new men'. This led to a famous row with his sister during which he suggested with scornful irony that if she were so desirous of political influence she would be better off becoming the king's mistress (a joke which did him no good at his trial). She felt he was trying to ruin her life, and Norfolk was none too pleased at the way Surrey had spoiled his best-laid plans. The testimony of his sister against him at his trial, and his father's unhelpful attitude, can probably be put down to this incident. The failure to create a Howard-Seymour alliance was a direct cause of his death.

Surrey was still apparently in the king's favour. He was given a high position at the elaborate peace treaty ceremonies in August; but when he returned to court after a stay in Norfolk, during which period the king had become seriously ill, the atmosphere was one of intense intrigue, for the nine-year-old Prince Edward would obviously be controlled by a regent when he succeeded to the throne, and the question was whether this would be Norfolk or Hertford.

Surrey was arrested towards the end of that year, denounced by his friend Sir Richard Southwell, who claimed that Surrey had placed in the first quarter of his heraldic shield the royal arms of England (which would imply a direct right to the English crown). There was no evidence whatsoever that he had done this, so the charge was changed to that of having borne in his escutcheon the royal arms ascribed to Edward the Confessor (to which Surrey had a legal right). When he was summoned before Council on December 2 he laughed at the absurdity of these charges and requested a trial, whereby he would demonstrate his innocence. Aware, however, that trials ended inevitably in conviction, he changed this to a request for trial by combat, offering to fight 'in his shirt' while his accuser wore armour (a superficial look at Surrey's life does make one marvel at the accuracy of the Hollywood portrayal of medieval England). This was refused. Norfolk was also arrested on December 12, and he confessed to high treason in concealing the false and traitorous act of his son (i.e., using the arms of Edward the Confessor to which he had a legal right). Before condemning Norfolk too harshly one must bear in mind the Stalinist atmosphere of the English court at that time, and assume he thought the only way to save his son was by obtaining royal pardon. As the French ambassador said: 'When a man is imprisoned in the Tower none dare meddle with his affairs, unless to speak ill of him, for fear of being suspected of the same crime.'

Surrey's trial was held in the great hall of the Guildhall on Thursday, 13 January 1547. He is said to have held forth with wit and vigour from nine until five. He was condemned to be hanged, drawn and quartered like a common criminal, but this was later changed to execution by the axe at Tower Hill, which took place on January 19. Only the death of Henry VIII on January 27 saved Norfolk, who remained in the Tower until 1553.

Historians usually refer to Surrey, if at all, as an anachronism, a man with no grasp of how contemporary politics worked, possessing outmoded ideas of chivalry and honour, and an excessive belief in his own worth. For someone of his social rank, however, a belief in one's own worth was an inevitable part of life, and it seems truer to think of him as a virtuous man living in evil times. The demand for more 'realism' in his behaviour would also have to condemn his unique habit, when campaigning in France, of not putting women and children to the sword, as a failure to grasp the nature of contemporary military tactics and objectives. Henry VIII's decision to have him eliminated was probably not so much related to his character as to his having a claim to the throne (a better one than Henry's own, for that matter). Since the Seymours had no such claim they were a safer bet for the continuation of his line, with the

14

result that the country was left 'in the hands of the most un-principled gang of political adventurers and predators England had seen for many centuries' (W.G. Hoskins, *The Age of Plunder: King Henry's England, 1500-1547* (1976).

Surrey's lack of a champion among historians is paralleled by his lack of support among literary critics this century, and even during the nineteenth his reputation was in slow decline, while still staying higher than that of Wyatt. The anonymous reviewer in the *Edinburgh Review*, 1816, of Nott's great edition of Surrey and Wyatt may have totally dismissed any claim Wyatt may have had to be considered a poet and devoted most of his space to Surrey, but still his opinion of Surrey was only very low. In W.J. Courthope's *A History of English Poetry* (1895-1910) Wyatt was finally praised by somebody, although Surrey was still considered the more important of the two; but the twentieth century saw a complete reversal in Wyatt's fortunes, and the last book to place Surrey above Wyatt was J.M. Berdan's *Early Tudor Poetry 1485-1547* in 1920. E.M.W. Tillyard and E.K. Chambers then proclaimed the new Wyatt of dramatic lyric spontaneity and striking non-traditional metres, and the job was done. Wyatt had been dismissed by the eighteenth century for the same reasons that the metaphysical poets had been condemned, and now the wheel had come full circle, Surrey being rejected for the 'correctness' which the eighteenth century had praised.

Fashion should not be allowed to play so large a role in the evaluation of two poets who are not in competition with each other and whose value should be by now above question. Surrey is no precursor of Waller any more than Wyatt is the poor man's Donne. The few lines of Pope I have quoted here should be a reminder, if any were needed, that the movement of Surrey's verse is quite different from that of the eighteenth century. Surrey is out of fashion because the bare purity of his diction and the stable structure of his poetic form will not respond to the crude tools of critical analysis which have been so much used and misused this century; but that is our fault and not

15

his. He also lacks the sense of conflict which pervades Wyatt's poetry, Surrey's basic poetic world being one of emotional acceptance rather than strife, a passive apprehension of the real which is as valuable as any drama of action. In these two poets we can see the two poles of human experience upon which a sane world would turn. We need both these poets, and it is time we listened again to the one we have closed our ears to for so long.

Textual and bibliographical note

Manuscripts of Surrey's poems exist (the editions of Padelford (1920) and Jones (1964) are based on them) but they have no real authority since there is nothing in Surrey's hand and they all seem to be later than the first printed versions. I have made use of the two above editions, and also that of Nott (1815) and Tottel (1557), choosing those readings which seemed right to me. This is not a critical edition so I have not felt the need to justify, or even indicate, my choices. The text is, however, fairly close to Jones, to whom I acknowledge a considerable debt, although the spelling has been modernized in accordance with Fyfield Books policy.

There is a standard biography by Edwin Casady (1938). This is standard because it is the only one. Despite the deterministic flourishes in the opening pages ('Free will is a myth...', 'any man's actions are largely predetermined...', 'result of changing economic conditions...') expectations of some Freudo-Marxist study are soon disappointed, and the book is straightforward and pedestrian enough, indeed amazingly dull considering how interesting Surrey's life was. Hester V. Chapman in *Two Tudor Portraits* (1960) demonstrates she has a sharper mind than Casady, but she is so unsympathetic towards her subject as to be malicious, and one ends by questioning her motives in writing such a book. There is no book-length critical study of Surrey's poetry. Clyde W. Jentoft, *Sir Thomas Wyatt and Henry Howard, Earl of Surrey: a reference guide* (1980), besides giving much sensible and well-organized information, which I have found very helpful, lists all the available reading; but Surrey is just as much in need of good criticism as he is of a definitive, complete editing, and there is nothing I can recommend with enthusiasm.

Finally I apologize for the amount of notes, which is not in accordance with Fyfield policy at all, but this poet will read better if set in a context where the integrity of his work as a whole can be grasped, and he can then be seen as much more than the author of one or two half-forgotten anthology pieces.

Virgil's Aeneid

1 *Book II, lines 1-73*

> They whisted all, with fixed face attent
> When prince Aeneas from the royal seat
> Thus gan to speak: O Queen, it is thy will
> I should renew a woe cannot be told,
> How that the Greeks did spoil and overthrow   5
> The Phrygian wealth and wailful realm of Troy,
> Those ruthful things that I myself beheld,
> And whereof no small part fell to my share.
> Which to express, who could refrain from tears?
> What Myrmidon? or yet what Dolopes?   10
> What stern Ulysses' wagèd soldiar?
> And lo, moist night now from the welkin falls,
> And stars declining counsel us to rest,
> But since so great is thy delight to hear
> Of our mishaps, and Troia's last decay,   15
> Though to record the same my mind abhors
> And plaint eschews, yet thus will I begin.
> The Greeks' chieftains, all irkèd with the war
> Wherein they wasted had so many years
> And oft repulsed by fatal destiny,   20
> A huge horse made, high raisèd like a hill,
> By the divine science of Minerva;
> Of cloven fir compacted were his ribs;
> For their return a feignèd sacrifice,
> The fame whereof so wandered it at point.   25
> In the dark bulk they closed bodies of men
> Chosen by lot, and did enstuff by stealth
> The hollow womb with armèd soldiars.
> There stands in sight an isle hight Tenedon,
> Rich and of fame while Priam's kingdom stood;   30
> Now but a bay, and road unsure for ship.

Hither them secretly the Greeks withdrew
Shrouding themselves under the desert shore.
And, weening we they had been fled and gone,
And with that wind had fet the land of Greece,   35
Troia discharged her long continued dole.
The gates cast up, we issued out to play,
The Greekish camp desirous to behold,
The places void and the forsaken coasts.
Here Pyrrhus' band, their fierce Achilles' pight;   40
Here rode their ships, there did their battles join.
Astonied some the scatheful gift beheld,
Behight by vow unto the chaste Minerve,
All wondering at the hugeness of the horse.
      And first of all Timoetes gan advise   45
Within the walls to lead and draw the same,
And place it eke amid the palace court:
Whether of guile, or Troia's fate it would.
Capys, with some of judgment more discreet,
Willed it to drown, or underset with flame   50
The suspect present of the Greeks' deceit,
Or bore and gauge the hollow caves uncouth.
So diverse ran the giddy people's mind.
      Lo, foremost of a rout that followed him,
Kindled Laocoön hasted from the tower,   55
Crying far off: 'O wretched citizens,
What so great kind of frenzy fretteth you?
Deem ye the Greeks our enemies to be gone?
Or any Greekish gifts can you suppose
Devoid of guile? Is so Ulysses known?   60
Either the Greeks are in this timber hid,
Or this an engine is to annoy our walls,
To view our towers, and overwhelm our town.
Here lurks some craft. Good Trojans, give no trust
Unto this horse, for whatsoever it be,   65
I dread the Greeks, yea, when they offer gifts.'
And with that word, with all his force a dart

20

He lancèd then into that crooked womb;
Which trembling stuck, and shook within the side,
Wherewith the caves gan hollowly resound.   70
And but for Fates and for our blind forecast,
The Greeks' device and guile had been descried,
Troy yet had stand, and Priam's towers so high.

2   *Book II, lines 295-462*

We cleft the walls and closures of the town   295
Whereto all help, and underset the feet
With sliding rolls, and bound his neck with ropes.
This fatal gin thus overclamb our walls,
Stuffed with armed men, about the which there ran
Children and maids that holy carols sang;   300
And well were they whose hands might touch the cords.
With threatening cheer thus slided through our town
The subtil tree, to Pallas' temple-ward.
O native land! Ilion! and of the gods
The mansion place! O warlike walls of Troy!   305
Four times it stopped in th' entry of our gate,
Four times the harness clattered in the womb.
But we go on, unsound of memory,
And blinded eke by rage persever still.
This fatal monster in the fane we place.   310
        Cassandra then, inspired with Phoebus' sprite,
Her prophet's lips, yet never of us leeved,
Disclosèd eft, forespeaking things to come.
We wretches, lo, that last day of our life,
With boughs of fest the town and temples deck.   315
        With this the sky gan whirl about the sphere;
The cloudy night gan thicken from the sea,
With mantles spread that cloakèd earth and skies
And eke the treason of the Greekish guile.
The watchmen lay dispersed, to take their rest,   320

21

Whose wearied limbs sound sleep had then oppressed.
When well in order comes the Grecian fleet
From Tenedon, towards the coasts well known,
By friendly silence of the quiet moon.
When the king's ship put forth his mark of fire, 325
Sinon, preserved by froward destiny,
Let forth the Greeks enclosèd in the womb;
The closures eke of pine by stealth unpinned
Whereby the Greeks restorèd were to air,
With joy down hasteing from the hollow tree. 330
With cords let down did slide unto the ground
The great captains: Sthenel, and Thessander,
The fierce Ulysses, Athamos, and Thoas,
Machaon first, and then King Menalae,
Epeus eke that did the engine forge; 335
And straight invade the town yburied then
With wine and sleep. And first the watch is slain,
The gates unfold to let their fellows in:
They join themselves with the conjurèd bands.
    It was the time when, granted from the gods, 340
The first sleep creeps most sweet in weary folk.
Lo, in my dream before mine eyes, methought
With rueful cheer I saw where Hector stood,
Out of whose eyes there gushèd streams of tears,
Drawn at a cart as he of late had be, 345
Distained with bloody dust, whose feet were bowln
With the strait cords wherewith they halèd him.
Ay me, what one! that Hector how unlike
Which erst returned clad with Achilles' spoils,
Or when he threw into the Greekish ships 350
The Trojan flame! so was his beard defiled,
His crispèd locks all clustered with his blood,
With all such wounds as many he received
About the walls of that his native town.
Whom frankly thus methought I spake unto, 355
With bitter tears and doleful, deadly voice:

22

'O Trojan light! O only hope of thine!
What lets so long thee stayed? or from what coasts,
Our most desired Hector, dost thou come?
Whom, after slaughter of thy many friends,   360
And travail of thy people and thy town,
All-wearied, lord, how gladly we behold!
What sorry chance hath stained thy lively face?
Or why see I these wounds, alas so wide?'
He answered nought, nor in my vain demands   365
Abode, but from the bottom of his breast
Sighing he said: 'Flee, flee, O goddess' son,
And save thee from the fury of this flame.
Our enemies now are masters of the walls,
And Troia town now falleth from the top.   370
Sufficeth that is done for Priam's reign.
If force might serve to succour Troia town,
This right hand well might have been her defence.
But Troia now commendeth to thy charge
Her holy relics and her privy gods.   375
Them join to thee, as fellows of thy fate.
Large walls rear thou for them: for so thou shalt,
After time spent in the o'erwandered flood.'
This said, he brought forth Vesta in his hands,
Her fillets eke, and everlasting flame.   380
       In this meanwhile, with diverse plaint the town
Throughout was spread; and louder more and more
The din resounèd, with rattling of arms
(Although mine old father Anchises' house
Removèd stood, with shadow hid of trees).   385
I waked; therewith to the house top I clamb,
And hearkening stood I: like as when the flame
Lights in the corn by drift of boisteous wind,
Or the swift stream that driveth from the hill
Roots up the fields and presseth the ripe corn   390
And ploughèd ground, and overwhelms the grove,
The silly herdsman all astonied stands,

23

From the high rock while he doth hear the sound.
  Then the Greeks' faith, then their deceit appeared.
Of Deiphobus the palace large and great   395
Fell to the ground, all overspread with flash;
His next neighbour Ucalegon afire:
The Sygean seas did glister all with flame.
Up sprang the cry of men and trumpets' blast.
Then, as distraught, I did my armour on,   400
Nor could I tell yet whereto arms availed.
But with our feres to throng out from the press
Toward the tower our hearts brent with desire.
Wrath pricked us forth, and unto us it seemed
A seemly thing to die armed in the field.   405
  Wherewith Panthus, 'scaped from the Greekish darts,
Otreus' son, Phoebus' priest, brought in hand
The sacred relics and the vanquished gods,
And in his hand his little nephew led;
And thus, as frantic, to our gates he ran.   410
'Panthus,' quod I, 'In what estate stand we?
Or for refuge what fortress shall we take?'
Scarce spake I this when wailing thus he said:
'The latter day and fate of Troy is come,
The which no plaint or prayer may avail.   415
Trojans we were, and Troia was sometime,
And of great fame the Teucrian glory erst:
Fierce Jove to Greece hath now transposèd all.
The Greeks are lords over this fired town.
Yonder huge horse that stands amid our walls   420
Sheds armèd men; and Sinon, victor now,
With scorn of us doth set all things on flame.
And, rushèd in at our unfolded gates,
Are thousands more than ever came from Greece.
And some with weapons watch the narrow streets, 425
With bright swords drawn, to slaughter ready bent.
And scarce the watches of the gate began
Them to defend, and with blind fight resist.'

Through Panthus' words, and lightning of the gods
Amid the flame and arms ran I in press,   430
As fury guided me, and where as I had heard
The cry greatest that made the air resound.
Into our band then fell old Iphytus,
And Rhipeus, that met us by moonlight;
Dyman and Hypanis joining to our side,   435
With young Chorebus, Mygdonius' son,
Which in those days at Troia did arrive
Burning with rage of dame Cassandra's love,
In Priam's aid and rescue of his town.
Unhappy he, that would no credit give   440
Unto his spouse's words of prophecy.
    Whom when I saw assembled in such wise
So desperately the battle to desire,
Then furthermore thus said I unto them:
'O ye young men, of courage stout in vain,   445
For nought ye strive to save the burning town.
What cruel fortune hath betid, ye see;
The gods out of the temples all are fled,
Through whose might long this empire was maintained;
Their altars eke are left both waste and void.   450
But if your will be bent with me to prove
That uttermost that now may us befall,
Then let us die, and run amid our foes.
To vanquished folk despair is only hope.'
    With this the young men's courage did increase,   455
And through the dark, like to the ravening wolves
Whom raging fury of their empty maws
Drives from their den, leaving with hungry throats
Their whelps behind, among our foes we ran,
Upon their swords, unto apparent death;   460
Holding alway the chief street of the town,
Covered with the close shadows of the night.

And now we gan draw near unto the gate,
Right well escaped the danger, as methought,
When that at hand a sound of feet we heard.
My father then, gazing throughout the dark,
Crièd on me, 'Flee, son! They are at hand.'   970
With that bright shields and sheen armours I saw.
But then I know not what unfriendly god
My troubled wit from me bereft for fear;
For while I ran by the most secret streets,
Eschewing still the common haunted track,   975
From me caitiff, alas, bereavèd was
Creüsa then, my spouse, I wot not how,
Whether by fate, or missing of the way,
Or that she was by weariness retained.
But never sith these eyes might her behold,   980
Not did I yet perceive that she was lost,
Nor never backward turnèd I my mind,
Till we came to the hill where as there stood
The old temple dedicate to Ceres.

    And when that we were there assembled all,   985
She was only away, deceiving us,
Her spouse, her son, and all her company.
What god or man did I not then accuse,
Near wood for ire? or what more cruel chance
Did hap to me in all Troy's overthrow?   990
Ascanius to my feres I then betook,
With Anchises, and eke the Trojan gods,
And left them hid within a valley deep.
And to the town I gan me hie again,
Clad in bright arms, and bent for to renew   995
Adventures past, to search throughout the town,
And yield my head to perils once again.

    And first the walls and dark entry I sought
Of the same gate where as I issued out,

Holding backwards the steps where we had come,   1000
In the dark night, looking all round about.
In every place the ugsome sights I saw,
The silence self of night aghast my sprite.
From hence again I passed unto our house,
If she by chance had been returnèd home.   1005
The Greeks were there, and had it all beset:
The wasting fire blown up by drift of wind
Above the roofs; the blazing flame sprang up,
The sound whereof with fury pierced the skies.
To Priam's palace and the castle then   1010
I made; and there at Juno's sanctuary,
In the void porches, Phoenix, Ulysses eke,
Stern guardians stood, watching of the spoil.
The riches here were set, reft from the brent
Temples of Troy; the tables of the gods,   1015
The vessels eke that were of massy gold,
And vestures spoiled, were gathered all in heap.
The children orderly, and mothers pale for fright,
Long rangèd on a row stood round about.
    So bold was I to show my voice that night,   1020
With clepes and cries to fill the streets throughout,
With Creüsa's name in sorrow, with vain tears,
And oftensithes the same for to repeat.
The town restless with fury as I sought,
Th'unlucky figure of Creüsa's ghost,   1025
Of stature more than wont, stood fore mine eyes.
Abashèd then I woxe. Therewith my hair
Gan start right up, my voice stuck in my throat.
When with such words she gan my heart remove:
'What helps to yield unto such furious rage,   1030
Sweet spouse?' quod she. 'Without will of the gods
This chancèd not; nor lawful was for thee
To lead away Creüsa hence with thee:
The king of the high heaven suffreth it not.
A long exile thou art assigned to bear,   1035

27

Long to furrow large space of stormy seas:
So shalt thou reach at last Hesperian land,
Where Lydian Tiber with his gentle stream
Mildly doth flow along the fruitful fields.
There mirthful wealth, there kingdom is for thee,   1040
There a king's child prepared to be thy make.
For thy beloved Creüsa stint thy tears:
For now I shall not see the proud abodes
Of Myrmidons, nor yet of Dolopes;
Nor I, a Trojan lady and the wife   1045
Unto the son of Venus the goddess,
Shall go a slave to serve the Greekish dames.
Me here the god's great mother holds.
And now farewell, and keep in father's breast
The tender love of thy young son and mine.'   1050
    This having said, she left me all in tears,
And minding much to speak; but she was gone,
And subtly fled into the weightless air.
Thrice raught I with my arms t'accoll her neck,
Thrice did my hands vain hold th'image escape   1055
Like nimble winds, and like the flying dream.
So night spent out, return I to my feres;
And there wand'ring I find together swarmed
A new number of mates, mothers and men,
A rout exiled, a wretched multitude,   1060
From eachwhere flocked together, pressed to pass,
With heart and goods, to whatsoever land
By sliding seas me listed them to lead.
And now rose Lucifer above the ridge
Of lusty Ide, and brought the dawning light.   1065
The Greeks held th'entries of the gates beset;
Of help there was no hope. Then gave I place,
Took up my sire, and hasted to the hill.

28

But now the wounded queen with heavy care,
Throughout the veins she nourisheth the playe,
Surprisèd with blind flame; and to her mind
Gan eke resort the prowess of the man
And honour of his race; while in her breast   5
Imprinted stack his words and picture's form:
Nor to her limbs care granteth quiet rest.
    The next morrow with Phoebus' lamp the earth
Alightened clear, and eke the dawning day
The shadows dank gan from the pole remove,   10
When all unsound her sister of like mind
Thus spake she to: 'O sister Anne, what dreams
Be these, that me tormented thus affray?
What new guest this that to our realm is come?
What one of cheer! How stout of heart in arms!   15
Truly I think, nor vain is my belief,
Of goddish race some offspring should he be:
Cowardry notes hearts swervèd out of kind.
He driven, Lord, with how hard destiny!
What battles eke achievèd did he tell!   20
But that my mind is fixed unmoveably
Never with wight in wedlock aye to join
Sith my first love me left by death dissevered,
If genial brands and bed me loathèd not,
To this one guilt perchance yet might I yield.   25
Anne, for I grant, since wretched Sychaeus' death,
My spouse, and house with brother's slaughter stained,
This only man hath made my senses bend
And prickèd forth my mind that gan to slide.
Now feelingly I taste the steps of mine old flame.   30
But first I wish the earth me swallow down
With thunder, or the mighty lord me send
To the pale ghosts of hell and darkness deep,
Ere I thee stain, shamefastness, or thy laws.

29

He that with me first coupled took away   35
My love with him, enjoys it in his grave.'
     Thus did she say, and with surprisèd tears
Bainèd her breast. Whereto Anne thus replied:
'O sister, dearer beloved than the light,
Thy youth alone in plaint still wilt thou spill,   40
That children sweet nor Venus' gifts doth know?
Doth dust, think'st thou, mind this? or gravèd ghosts?
Time of thy dole, thy spouse new dead, I grant
None might thee move: no, not the Libyan king,
Nor yet of Tyre, Iarbas set so light,   45
And other princes more whom the rich soil
Of Afric breeds in honours triumphant.
Wilt thou also gainstand thy likèd love?
Comes not to mind upon whose land thou dwell'st?
On this side, lo the Getule town behold,   50
A people bold, unvanquishèd in war;
And the undaunted Numides compass thee,
With Sirtes, the unfriendly harbour,
On th'other hand, a desert realm for thirst,
The Barceans, whose fury stretches wide.   55
What shall I touch the wars that move from Tyre?
Or yet thy brother's threats?
By God's purveyance it blew, and Juno's help,
The Trojans' ships, I think, to run this course.
Sister, what town shalt thou see this become!   60
Through such ally how shall our kingdom rise!
And by the aid of Trojan arms how great!
How many ways shall Carthage's glory grow!
Thou only now beseech the gods of grace
By sacrifice: which ended, to thy house   65
Receive him, and forge causes of abode;
Whiles winter frets the seas, and watery Orion,
The ships shaken, unfriendly the season.'
     Such words enflamed the kindled mind with love,
Loosèd all shame, and gave the doubtful hope.   70

And to the temples first they haste, and seek
By sacrifice for grace, with hogrels of two years
Chosen, as ought, to Ceres that gave laws,
To Phoebus, Bacchus, and to Juno chief
Which hath in care the bonds of marriage.   75
Fair Dido held in her right hand the cup,
Which twixt the horns of a white cow she shed
In presence of the gods, passing before
The altars fat, which she renewèd oft
With gifts that day, and beasts debowellèd,   80
Gazing for counsel on the entrails warm.
Ay me, unskilful minds of prophecy!
Temples or vows, what boot they in her rage?
A gentle flame the marrow doth devour,
Whiles in her breast the silent wound keeps life.   85
Unhappy Dido burns, and in her rage
Throughout the town she wandreth up and down,
Like to the stricken hind with shaft in Crete,
Throughout the woods which chasing with his darts
Aloof, the shepherd smites at unawares   90
And leaves unwist in her the thirling head,
That through the groves and lands glides in her flight;
Amid whose side the mortal arrow sticks.
      Aeneas now about the wall she leads,
The town prepared and Carthage wealth to show.   95
Offering to speak, amid her voice, she whists.
And when the day gan fail, now feasts she makes;
The Trojans' travails to hear anew she lists
Enragèd all, and stareth in his face
That tells the tale. And when they were all gone,   100
And the dim moon doth oft withhold the light
And sliding stars provokèd unto sleep,
Alone she mourns within her palace void,
And sits her down on her forsaken bed.
And absent him she hears, when he is gone,   105
And seeth eke. Oft in her lap she holds

31

Ascanius, trapped by his father's form,
So to beguile the love cannot be told.

5 *Book IV, lines 359-518*

    Aeneas, with that vision stricken down,
Well near bestraught, upstart his hair for dread,   360
Amid his throat his voice likewise gan stick.
For to depart by flight he longeth now,
And the sweet land to leave, astonied sore
With this advice and message of the gods.
What may he do, alas? or by what words   365
Dare he persuade the raging queen in love?
Or in what sort may he his tale begin?
Now here, now there, his reckless mind gan run
And diversely him draws, discussing all.
After long doubts this sentence seemèd best: 370
Mnestheus first, and strong Cloanthus eke,
He calls to him, with Sergest; unto whom
He gave in charge his navy secretly
For to prepare, and drive to the sea coast
His people, and their armour to address,   375
And for the cause of change to feign excuse;
And that he, when good Dido least foreknew
Or did suspect so great a love could break,
Would wait his time to speak thereof most meet,
The nearest way to hasten his intent.   380
Gladly his will and biddings they obey.
    Full soon the queen this crafty sleight can smell,
(Who can deceive a lover in forecast?)
And first foresaw the motions for to come,
Things most assurèd fearing; unto whom   385
That wicked Fame reported how to flight
Was armed the fleet, all ready to avail.
Then ill bestead of counsel rageth she,

And whisketh through the town like Bacchus' nun,
As Thyas stirs, the sacred rites begun,   390
And when the wonted third year's sacrifice
Doth prick her forth, hearing Bacchus' name hallowed,
And that the festful night of Citheron
Doth call her forth with noises of dauncing.
    At length her self bordeth Aeneas thus: 395
'Unfaithful wight, to cover such a fault
Couldest thou hope? unwist to leave my land?
Not thee our love, nor yet right hand betrothed,
Nor cruel death of Dido may withhold?
But that thou wilt in winter ships prepare   400
And try the seas in broil of whorling winds?
What if the land thou seekest were not strange,
If not unknown, or ancient Troia stood,
In rough seas yet should Troia town be sought?
Shunnest thou me? By these tears and right hand   405
(For nought else have I wretched left myself),
By our spousals and marriage begun,
If I of thee deservèd ever well,
Or thing of mine were ever to thee lief,
Rue on this realm whose ruin is at hand!   410
If aught be left that prayer may avail,
I thee beseech to do away this mind.
The Libyans, and tyrans of Numidan,
For thee me hate; my Tyrians eke for thee
Are wroth; by thee my shamefastness eke stained,   415
And good renown, whereby up to the stars
Peerless I claim. To whom wilt thou me leave,
Ready to die, my sweet guest? sith this name
Is all as now that of a spouse remains.
But whereto now should I prolong my death?   420
What? until my brother Pygmalion
Beat down my walls? or the Getulian
Hyarbas yet captive lead me away?
Before thy flight a child had I conceived,

33

Or seen a young Aeneas in my court   425
Play up and down, that did present thy face,
All utterly I could not seem forsaken.'
        Thus said the queen. He, to the god's advice,
Unmovèd held his eyes, and in his breast
Repressed his care, and strove against his will.   430
And these few words at last then forth he cast:
'Never shall I deny, queen, thy desert
Greater than thou in words may well express.
To think on thee ne irk me aye it shall
Whiles of my self I shall have memory,   435
And whiles the spirit these limbs of mine shall rule.
For present purpose somewhat shall I say.
Never meant I to cloak the same by stealth
(Slander me not), nor to escape by flight.
Nor I to thee pretended marriage,   440
Nor hither came to join me in such league.
If destiny at mine own liberty
To lead my life would have permitted me,
After my will my sorrow to redub,
Troy, and the remainder of our folk,   445
Restore I should, and with these escaped hands
The walls again unto the vanquishèd,
And palace high of Priam eke repair.
But now Apollo callèd Grineus
And prophecies of Licia me advise   450
To seize upon the realm of Italy:
That is my love, my country, and my land.
If Carthage turrets thee, Phoenician born,
And of a Libyan town the sight detain,
To us Trojans why dost thou then envy   455
In Italy to make our residence?
Lawful is eke for us strange realms to seek.
As oft as night doth cloak with shadows dank
The earth, as oft as flaming stars appear,
The troubled ghost of my father Anchises   460

34

So oft in sleep doth fray me and advise
The wrongèd head by me of my dear son,
Whom I defraud of the Hisperian crown
And lands allotted him by destiny.
The messenger eke of the gods but late   465
Sent down by Jove (I swear by either head)
Passing the air, did this to me report.
In bright daylight the god myself I saw
Enter these walls, and with these ears him heard.
Leave then with plaint to vex both thee and me.   470
Against my will to Italy I go.'
        Whiles in this sort he did this tale pronounce,
With wayward look she gan him aye behold,
And rolling eyes that movèd to and fro,
With silent look discoursing over all.   475
And forth in rage at last thus gan she braid:
'Faithless, forsworn, no goddess was thy dam
Nor Dardanus beginner of thy race,
But of hard rocks Mount Caucase monstruous
Bred thee, and teats of tigers gave thee suck.   480
But what should I dissemble now my cheer?
Or me reserve to hope of greater things?
Minds he our tears? or ever moved his eyes?
Wept he for ruth? or pitied he our love?
What should I set before? or where begin?   485
Juno nor Jove with just eyes this beholds.
There is no faith, no surety to be found.
Did I not him, thrown up upon my shore,
In need receive, and funded eke invest
Of half my realm? his navy lost repair?   490
From death's danger his fellows eke defend?
Ay me, with rage and furies am I drive!
Apollo now, now Lycian prophecies,
Another while the messenger of gods
(He says) sent down from mighty Jove himself,   495
The dreadful charge amid the skies hath brought.

35

As though that were the travail of the gods,
Or such a care their quietness might move.
I hold thee not, nor yet gainsay thy words:
To Italy pass on by help of winds,   500
And through the floods go search thy kingdom new.
If ruthful gods have any power, I trust
Amid the rocks thy guerdon thou shalt find,
When thou shalt clepe full oft on Dido's name.
With burial brands I absent shall thee chase,   505
And when cold death from life these limbs divides,
My ghost eachwhere shall still on thee await.
Thou shalt abye, and I shall hear thereof;
Among the souls below thy bruit shall come.'
        With suchlike words she cut off half her tale,   510
With pensive heart abandoning the light,
And from his sight herself gan far remove,
Forsaking him that many things in fear
Imaginèd, and did prepare to say.
Her swooning limbs her damsels gan relieve,   515
And to her chamber bore of marble stone,
And laid her on her bed with tapets spread.

6 *Book IV, lines 780-884*

        Aurora now from Titan's purple bed   780
With new daylight hath overspread the earth,
When by her windows the queen the peeping day
Espied, and navy with splayed sails depart
The shore, and eke the port of vessels void.
Her comely breast three or four times she smote   785
With her own hand, and tore her golden tress.
'Oh Jove,' quoth she, 'shall he then thus depart
A stranger thus and scorn our kingdom so?
Shall not my men do on their armour prest,
And eke pursue them throughout all the town?   790

36

Out of the road soon shall the vessels warp.
Haste on, cast flame, set sail and wield your oars!
What said I? But where am I? What frenzy
Alters thy mind, unhappy Dido? now
Hath thee beset a froward destiny.   795
Then it behove, when thou with him divid'st
The sceptre, lo, his faith and his right hand,
That leads with him, they say, his country gods,
That on his back his aged father bore.
His body might I not have caught and rent?   800
And in the seas drenchèd him and his feres?
And from Ascanius his life with iron reft,
And set him on his father's board for meat?
Of such debate perchance the fortune might
Have been doubtful; would god it were assayed!   805
Whom should I fear, sith I myself must die?
Might I have thrown into that navy brands,
And fillèd eke their decks with flaming fire,
The father, son, and all their nation
Destroyed, and fall'n myself dead over all.   810
Sun, with thy beams that mortal works descries,
And thou Juno, that well these travails knowest,
Proserpine thou, upon whom folk do use
To howl, and call in forkèd ways by night,
Infernal furies, ye wreakers of wrong,   815
And Dido's gods, who stand at point of death,
Receive these words, and eke your heavy power
Withdraw from me, that wicked folk deserve,
And our request accept, we you beseech.
If so that yonder wicked head must needs   820
Recover port, and sail to land of force,
And if Jove's will have so resolvèd it
And such end set as no wight can fordo,
Yet at the least assailèd might he be
With arms and wars of hardy nations,   825
From the bounds of his kingdom far exiled,

37

Iulus eke ravished out of his arms,
Driven to call for help, that he may see
The guiltless corpses of his folk lie dead.
And after hard conditions of peace,   830
His realm nor life desired may he brook,
But fall before his time, ungraved amid the sands.
This I require, these words with blood I shed.
And Tyrians, ye his stock and all his race
Pursue with hate, reward our cinders so.   835
No love or league betwixt our peoples be,
And of our bones some wreaker may there spring,
With sword and flame that Trojans may pursue.
And from henceforth, when that our power may stretch,
Our coasts to them contrary be for aye,   840
I crave of God, and our streams to their floods,
Arms unto arms, and offspring of each race,
With mortal war each other may fordo.'
     This said, her mind she writhèd on all sides,
Seeking with speed to end this irksome life.   845
To Sychaeus' nurse Barcen then thus she said
(For her's at home in ashes did remain):
'Call unto me, dear nurse, my sister Anne.
Bid her in haste in water of the flood
She sprinkle the body, and bring the beasts   850
And purging sacrifice I did her show.
So let her come; and thou thy temples bind
With sacred garlands; for the sacrifice
That I to Pluto have begun, my mind
Is to perform, and give end to these cares;   855
And Trojan statue throw into the flame.'
When she had said, redouble gan her nurse
Her steps, forth on an agèd woman's trot.
     But trembling Dido eagerly now bent
Upon her stern determination,   860
Her bloodshot eyes rolling within her head,
Her quivering cheeks fleckèd with deadly stain,

Both pale and wan to think on death to come,
Into the inward wards of her palace
She rusheth in, and clamb up as distraught   865
The burial stack, and drew the Trojan sword,
Her gift sometime, but meant to no such use.
Where when she saw his weed and well known bed,
Weeping a while, in study gan she stay,
Fell on the bed, and these last words she said: 870
'Sweet spoils, while God and destiny did permit,
Receive this spirit, and rid me of these cares.
I lived and ran the course fortune did grant,
And under earth my great ghost now shall wend.
A goodly town I built, and saw my walls,   875
Happy, alas too happy, if these coasts
The Trojan ships had never touchèd aye.'
      This said, she laid her mouth close to the bed.
'Why then,' quoth she, 'unwroken shall we die?
But let us die, for thus and in this sort   880
It liketh us to seek the shadows dark.
And from the seas the cruel Trojan's eyes
Shall well discern this flame, and take with him
Eke these unlucky tokens of my death.'

From the Italian

7

The soote season, that bud and bloom forth brings
With green hath clad the hill and eke the vale;
The nightingale with feathers new she sings;
And turtle to her make hath told her tale.
Summer is come, for every spray now springs;   5
The hart hath hung his old head on the pale;
The buck in brake his winter coat he flings;
The fishes flete with new repairèd scale;
The adder all her slough away she slings;
The swift swallow pursueth the flies small;   10
The busy bee her honey now she mings;
Winter is worn that was the flowers' bale.
And thus I see among these pleasant things
Each care decays, and yet my sorrow springs.

8

Set me where as the sun doth parch the green,
Or where his beams may not dissolve the ice;
In temperate heat where he is felt and seen;
With proud people, in presence sad and wise;
Set me in base, or yet in high degree,   5
In the long night, or in the shortest day,
In clear weather, or where mists thickest be,
In lost youth, or when my hairs be grey;
Set me in earth, in heaven, or yet in hell,
In hill, in dale, or in the foaming flood;   10
Thrall, or at large, alive where so I dwell,
Sick, or in health, in ill fame or in good:
Yours will I be, and with that only thought
Comfort myself when that my hope is nought.

9

Love that doth reign and live within my thought,
And built his seat within my captive breast,
Clad in the arms wherein with me he fought,
Oft in my face he doth his banner rest.
But she that taught me love and suffer pain,   5
My doubtful hope and eke my hot desire
With shamefast look to shadow and refrain,
Her smiling grace converteth straight to ire.
And coward love then to the heart apace
Taketh his flight, where he doth lurk and plain   10
His purpose lost, and dare not show his face.
For my lord's guilt thus faultless bide I pain;
Yet from my lord shall not my foot remove.
Sweet is the death that taketh end by love.

10

In Cyprus springs, where as dame Venus dwelt,
A well so hot that who so tastes the same,
Were he of stone, as thawèd ice should melt,
And kindled find his breast with secret flame;
Whose moist poison dissolvèd hath my hate.   5
This creeping fire my cold limbs so oppressed
That in the heart that harboured freedom late
Endless despair long thraldom hath impressed.
One eke so cold in frozen snow is found
Whose chilling venom of repugnant kind   10
The fervent heat doth quench of Cupid's wound,
And with the spot of change infects the mind;
Whereof my dear hath tasted to my pain.
My service thus is grown into disdain.

11

I never saw you, madam, lay apart
Your cornet black, in cold nor yet in heat,
Sith first you knew of my desire so great
Which other fancies chased clean from my heart.
Whiles to myself I did the thought reserve   5
That so unware did wound my woeful breast,
Pity I saw within your heart did rest;
But since ye knew I did you love and serve,
Your golden tress was clad alway in black,
Your smiling looks were hid thus evermore,   10
All that withdrawn that I did crave so sore.
So doth this cornet govern me alack,
In summer sun, in winter breath of frost;
Of your fair eyes whereby the light is lost.

12

Alas, so all things now do hold their peace,
Heaven and earth disturbèd in no thing;
The beasts, the air, the birds their song do cease;
The nightes car the stars about doth bring.
Calm is the sea, the waves work less and less.   5
So am not I, whom love, alas, doth wring,
Bringing before my face the great increase
Of my desires, whereat I weep and sing
In joy and woe as in a doubtful ease.
For my sweet thoughts sometime do pleasure bring,   10
But by and by the cause of my disease
Gives me a pang that inwardly doth sting,
When that I think what grief it is again
To live and lack the thing should rid my pain.

13

The golden gift that nature did thee give
To fasten friends and feed them at thy will
With form and favour, taught me to believe
How thou art made to show her greatest skill.
Whose hidden virtues are not so unknown,   5
But lively dooms might gather at the first
Where beauty so her perfect seed hath sown,
Of other graces follow needs there must.
Now certes, lady, since all this is true,
That from above thy gift are thus elect,   10
Do not deface them then with fancies new,
Nor change of minds let not thy mind infect;
But mercy him thy friend that does thee serve,
Who seeks alway thine honour to preserve.

14

The sun hath twice brought forth the tender green
And clad the earth in lively lustiness,
Once have the winds the trees despoilèd clean

And now again begins their cruelness,
Since I have hid under my breast the harm   5
That never shall recover healthfulness.

The winter's hurt recovers with the warm;
The parchèd green restorèd is with shade:
What warmth, alas, may serve for to disarm

The frozen heart that mine inflame hath made?   10
What cold again is able to restore
My fresh green years that wither thus and fade?

Alas, I see nothing has hurt so sore
But time sometime reduceth a return;
Yet time my harm increaseth more and more,   15

And seems to have my cure always in scorn.
Strange kind of death in life that I do try:
At hand to melt, far off in flame to burn;

And like as time list to my cure apply,
So doth each place my comfort clean refuse.   20
Each thing alive that sees the heaven with eye

With cloak of night may cover and excuse
Himself from travail of the day's unrest,
Save I, alas, against all others use,

That then stir up the torment of my breast   25
To curse each star as causer of my fate.
And when the sun hath eke the dark repressed

And brought the day, it doth nothing abate
The travail of my endless smart and pain.
For then, as one that hath the light in hate,   30

I wish for night, more covertly to plain
And me withdraw from every haunted place,
Lest in my cheer my chance should 'pear too plain;

And with my mind I measure, pace by pace,
To seek that place where I myself had lost,   35
That day that I was tangled in that lace,

In seeming slack that knitteth ever most;
But never yet the travail of my thought
Of better state could catch a cause to boast.

For if I find sometime that I have sought   40
Those stars by whom I trusted of the port,
My sails do fall, and I advance right nought,

As anchored fast; my sprites do all resort
To stand at gaze, and sink in more and more
The deadly harm which she doth take in sport.   45

Lo, if I seek, how I do find my sore!
And if I fly I carry with me still
The venomed shaft which doth his force restore

By haste of flight. And I may plain my fill
Unto my self, unless this careful song   50
Print in your heart some parcel of my will.

For I, alas, in silence all too long
Of mine old hurt yet feel the wound but green.
Rue on my life, or else your cruel wrong
Shall well appear, and by my death be seen.   55

15

Such wayward ways hath love that most part in discord;
Our wills do stand, whereby our hearts but seldom do accord.
Deceit is his delight, and to beguile and mock
The simple hearts which he doth strike with froward, diverse
    stroke.
He causeth hearts to rage with golden burning dart,   5
And doth allay with leaden cold again the other's heart.
Hot gleams of burning fire and easy sparks of flame
In balance of unequal weight he pondereth by aim.
From easy ford, where I might wade and pass full well
He me withdraws, and doth me drive into the dark deep well; 10
And me withholds where I am called and offered place,
And will that still my mortal foe I do beseech of grace.

He lets me to pursue a conquest well near won,
To follow where my pains were spilt or that my suit begun.
Lo, by these rules I know how soon a heart can turn   15
From war to peace, from truce to strife, and so again return.
I know how to convert my will in other's lust;
Of little stuff unto my self to weave a web of trust;
And how to hide my harm with soft, dissembled cheer,
When in my face the painted thoughts would outwardly
    appear.   20
I know how that the blood forsakes the face for dread,
And how by shame it stains again the cheek with flaming red.
I know under the green the serpent how he lurks;
The hammer of the restless forge I know eke how it works.
I know, and can by rote, the tale that I would tell,   25
But oft the words come forth awry of him that loveth well.
I know in heat and cold the lover how he shakes,
In singing how he can complain, in sleeping how he wakes
To languish without ache, sickless for to consume,
A thousand things for to devise resolving all his fume.   30
And though he lists to see his lady's face full sore,
Such pleasure as delights his eye doth not his health restore.
I know to seek the track of my desired foe,
And fear to find that I do seek: but chiefly this I know,
That lovers must transform into the thing beloved,   35
And live (alas, who could believe?) with sprite from life
    removed.
I know in hearty sighs and laughters of the spleen
At once to change my state, my will, and eke my colour clean.
I know how to deceive myself withouten help,
And how the lion chastised is by beating of the whelp.   40
In standing near my fire I know how that I freeze,
Far off to burn; in both to waste and so my life to lese.
I know how love doth rage upon the yielded mind,
How small a net may take and mesh a hart of gentle kind;
With seldom taste sweet to season heaps of gall,   45
Revivèd with a glimpse of grace old sorrows to let fall.

The hidden trains I know and secret snares of love;
How soon a look may print a thought that never will remove.
That slipper state I know, those sudden turns from wealth,
That doubtful hope, that certain woe, and sure despair of
   health.   50

16

Give place, ye lovers, here before
That spent your boasts and brags in vain;
My lady's beauty passeth more
The best of yours, I dare well sayen,
Than doth the sun the candle light,   5
Or brightest day the darkest night.

And therefore hath a troth as just
As had Penelope the fair,
For what she sayeth ye may it trust
As it by writing sealèd were,   10
And virtues hath she many moe
Than I with pen have skill to show.

I could rehearse, if that I would,
The whole effect of Nature's plaint,
When she had lost the perfect mould,   15
The like to whom she could not paint;
With wringing hands how she did cry,
And what she said, I know it, I.

I know she swore with raging mind,
Her kingdom only set apart,   20
There was no loss by law of kind
That could have gone so near her heart.
And this was chiefly all her pain,
She could not make the like again.

Sith Nature thus gave her the praise   25
To be the chiefest work she wrought,
In faith, methink some better ways
On your behalf might well be sought,

Than to compare, as ye have done,
To match the candle with the sun.   30

17

When Windsor walls sustained my wearied arm,
My hand my chin, to ease my restless head,
Each pleasant spot revested green with warm,
The blossomed boughs with lusty Ver yspread,
The flowered meads, the wedded birds so late,   5
Mine eyes discovered. Then did to mind resort
The jolly woes, the hateless short debate, —
The rakehell life that 'longs to love's disport.
Wherewith, alas, mine heavy charge of care
Heaped in my breast breaks forth against my will,   10
And smoky sighs that overcast the air.
My vapoured eyes such dreary tears distil
The tender spring to quicken where they fall,
And I half bent to throw me down withal.

18

So cruel a prison how could betide, alas,
As proud Windsor, where I, in lust and joy,
With a king's son my childish years did pass,
In greater feast than Priam's sons of Troy.

Where each sweet place returns a taste full sour.   5
The large green courts, where we were wont to hove,
With eyes cast up unto the maidens' tower,
And easy sighs, such as folk draw in love.

The stately sales, the ladies bright of hue,
The dances short, long tales of great delight,   10
With words and looks that tigers could but rue,
Where each of us did plead the other's right.

49

The palm play, where, despoilèd for the game,
With dazèd eyes oft we by gleams of love
Have missed the ball and got sight of our dame,   15
To bait her eyes which kept the leads above.

The gravelled ground, with sleeves tied on the helm,
On foaming horse, with swords and friendly hearts,
With cheer as though the one should overwhelm,
Where we have fought and chasèd oft with darts.   20

With silver drops the meads yet spread for ruth,
In active games of nimbleness and strength
Where we did strain, trailèd by swarms of youth,
Our tender limbs, that yet shot up in length.

The secret groves, which oft we made resound   25
Of pleasant plaint and of our ladies' praise,
Recording soft what grace each one had found,
What hope of speed, what dread of long delays.

The wild forest, the clothèd holts with green,
With reins availed and swift ybreathèd horse,   30
With cry of hounds and merry blasts between,
Where we did chase the fearful hart a force.

The void walls eke, that harboured us each night;
Wherewith, alas, revive within my breast
The sweet accord, such sleeps as yet delight,   35
The pleasant dreams, the quiet bed of rest,

The secret thoughts imparted with such trust,
The wanton talk, the diverse change of play,
The friendship sworn, each promise kept so just,
Wherewith we passed the winter nights away.   40

And with this thought the blood forsakes my face,
The tears berain my cheek of deadly hue;
The which, as soon as sobbing sighs, alas,
Upsuppèd have, thus I my plaint renew:

'O place of bliss, renewer of my woes,   45
Give me accompt where is my noble fere,
Whom in thy walls thou didst each night enclose,
To other lief, but unto me most dear.'

Each stone, alas, that doth my sorrow rue,
Returns thereto a hollow sound of plaint.   50
Thus I alone, where all my freedom grew,
In prison pine with bondage and restraint,

And with remembrance of the greater grief,
To banish the less I find my chief relief.

19
From Tuscan came my lady's worthy race;
Fair Florence was sometime her ancient seat;
The western isle, whose pleasant shore doth face
Wild Cambria's cliffs, did give her lively heat.
Fostered she was with milk of Irish breast;   5
Her sire an earl, her dame of prince's blood;
From tender years in Britain she doth rest,
With a king's child, where she tastes ghostly food.
Hunsdon did first present her to my eyen:
Bright is her hue, and Geraldine she hight: 10
Hampton me taught to wish her first for mine,
And Windsor, alas, doth chase me from her sight.
Beauty of kind, her virtues from above;
Happy is he that may obtain her love.

20

Though I regarded not
The promise made by me,
Or passèd not to spot
My faith and honesty,
Yet were my fancy strange   5
And wilful will to wite,
If I sought now to change
A falcon for a kite.

All men might well dispraise
My wit and enterprise,   10
If I esteemed a pease
Above a pearl in price,
Or judged the owl in sight
The sparhawk to excel,
Which flieth but in the night   15
As all men know right well;

Or, if I sought to sail
Into the brittle port,
Where anchor hold doth fail
To such as do resort,   20
And leave the haven sure
Where blows no blustering wind,
Nor fickleness in ure,
So far forth as I find.

No, think me not so light   25
Nor of so churlish kind,
Though it lay in my might
My bondage to unbind,
That I would leave the hind
To hunt the gander's foe.   30
No, no, I have no mind
To make exchanges so,

52

Nor yet to change at all:
For think it may not be
That I should seek to fall   35
From my felicity,
Desirous for to win,
And loath for to forgo,
Or new change to begin.
How may all this be so?   40

The fire it cannot freeze,
For it is not his kind,
Nor true love cannot lese
The constance of the mind;
Yet, as soon shall the fire   45
Want heat to blaze and burn,
As I in such desire
Have once a thought to turn.

21

Wrapped in my careless cloak, as I walk to and fro,
I see how love can show what force there reigneth in his bow;
And how he shooteth eke a hardy heart to wound;
And where he glanceth by again, that little hurt is found.
For seldom it is seen he woundeth hearts alike;   5
The one may rage when t'other's love is often far to seek.
All this I see, with more; and wonder thinketh me
How he can strike the one so sore, and leave the other free.
I see that wounded wight that suffreth all this wrong,
How he is fed with yeas and nays, and liveth all too long. 10
In silence though I keep such secrets to myself,
Yet do I see how she sometimes doth yield a look by stealth,
As though it seemed, 'Iwis, I will not lose thee so,'
When in her heart so sweet a thought did never truly grow.
Then say I thus: 'Alas, that man is far from bliss   15
That doth receive for his relief none other gain but this.

And she that feeds him so, I feel and find it plain,
Is but to glory in her power, that over such can reign.
Nor are such graces spent but when she thinks that he,
A wearied man, is fully bent such fancies to let free.   20
Then to retain him still, she wrasteth new her grace,
And smileth, lo, as though she would forthwith the man
    embrace.
But when the proof is made to try such looks withal,
He findeth then the place all void, and freighted full of gall.
Lord, what abuse is this! Who can such women praise   25
That for their glory do devise to use such crafty ways?
I that among the rest do sit and mark the row,
Find that in her is greater craft than is in twenty moe.
When tender years, alas, with wiles so well are sped,
What will she do when hoary hairs are powdered in her
    head?'   30

22

Girt in my guiltless gown, as I sit here and sew,
I see that things are not indeed as to the outward show.
And whoso list to look and note things somewhat near,
Shall find, where plainness seems to haunt, nothing but craft
    appear.
For with indifferent eyes myself can well discern   5
How some to guide a ship in storms stick not to take the stern;
Whose skill and cunning tried in calm to steer a barge,
They would soon show, you should soon see, it were too great
    a charge.
And some I see again sit still and say but small
That can do ten times more than they say they can do at all. 10
Whose goodly gifts are such, the more they understand,
The more they seek to learn and know and take less charge in
    hand.
And to declare more plain, the time flits not so fast
But I can bear right well in mind the song now sung and past.

The author whereof came, wrapped in a crafty cloak,   15
In will to force a flaming fire where he could raise no smoke.
If power and will had met, as it appeareth plain,
The truth nor right had ta'en no place, their virtues had been
    vain.
So that you may perceive, and I may safely see,
The innocent that guiltless is condemnèd should have be.   20
Much like untruth to this the story did declare,
Where th'elders laid to Susan's charge meet matter to compare.
They did her both accuse and eke condemn her too,
And yet no reason, right nor truth did lead them so to do.
And she thus judged to die, toward her death went forth   25
Fraughted with faith a patient pace, taking her wrong in worth.
But he that doth defend all those that in him trust,
Did raise a Child for her defense to shield her from th'unjust.
And Daniel chosen was then of this wrong to weet
How, in what place, and eke with whom she did this crime
    commit.   30
He caused the elders part the one from th'other's sight,
And did examine one by one and charged them both say right.
'Under a mulberry tree it was,' first said the one;
The next named a pomegranate tree, whereby the truth was
    known.
Then Susan was discharged, and they condemned to die,   35
As right requires and they deserve, that framed so foul a lie.
And he that her preserved, and let them of their lust,
Hath me defended hitherto, and will do still I trust.

23

Each beast can choose his fere according to his mind,
And eke can show a friendly cheer, like to their beastly kind.
A lion saw I late, as white as any snow,
Which seemèd well to lead the race, his port the same did show.
Upon the gentle beast to gaze it pleasèd me,   5
For still methought he seemèd well of noble blood to be.

And as he pranced before, still seeking for a make,
As who would say 'There is none here, I trow, will me forsake',
I might perceive a wolf as white as whale-his-bone,
A fairer beast, a fresher hue, beheld I never none,   10
Save that her looks were fierce and froward eke her grace.
Toward the which this gentle beast gan him advance apace,
And with a beck full low he bowèd at her feet
In humble wise, as who would say 'I am too far unmeet'.
But such a scornful cheer wherewith she him rewarded   15
Was never seen, I trow, the like, to such as well deservèd.
With that she start aside well near a foot or twain,
And unto him thus gan she say, with spite and great disdain:
'Lion,' she said, 'if thou hadst known my mind beforn,
Thou hadst not spent thy travail thus, nor all thy pain forlorn.   20
Do way! I let thee weet thou shalt not play with me:
Go range about, where thou mayst find some meeter fare for
     thee.'
Forthwith he beat his tail, his eyes began to flame;
I might perceive his noble heart much movèd by the same.
Yet saw I him refrain, and eke his wrath assuage,   25
And unto her thus gan he say, when he was past his rage:
'Cruel, you do me wrong to set me thus so light;
Without desert, for my good will, to show me such despite.
How can ye thus entreat a lion of the race,
That with his paws a crownèd king devoured in the place,   30
Whose nature is to prey upon no simple food,
As long as he may suck the flesh and drink of noble blood.
If you be fair and fresh, am I not of your hue?
And for my vaunt I dare well say my blood is not untrue.
For you yourself have heard, it is not long ago   35
Since that, for love, one of the race did end his life in woe.
In tower both strong and high, for his assurèd truth,
Where as in tears he spent his breath, alas, the more the ruth.
This gentle beast so died, whom nothing could remove,
But willingly to lose his life for loss of his true love.   40
Other there be whose life, to linger still in pain,

56

Against her will preservèd is that would have died right fain.
But well I might perceive that nought it moveth you,
My good intent, my gentle heart, nor yet my mind so true,
But that your will is such to lure me to the trade ~~pursue~~ 45
As other some full many years to trace by craft you made.
And thus behold my kind, how that we differ far:
I seek my foes, and you your friends do threaten still with war:
I fawn where I am fed, you flee that seeks to you;
I can devour no yielding prey, you kill where you subdue.   50
My kind is to desire the honour of the field,
And you with blood to slake your thirst on such as to you yield.
Wherefore I would you wist, that for your coy looks
I am no man that will be trained nor tangled by such hooks.
And though some list to bow where blame full well they
    might,   55
And do such beasts a currant fawn that should have travail
    bright,
I will observe the law that nature gave to me,
To conquer such as will resist, and let the rest go free.
And as a falcon free, that soareth in the air,
Which never fed on hand or lure, that for no stale doth care,   60
While that I live and breathe such shall my custom be,
In wildness of the woods to seek my prey where pleaseth me;
Where many one shall rue that never made offence:
Thus your refuse against my power shall bode them no defence.
In the revenge whereof I vow and swear thereto   65
A thousand spoils I shall commit I never thought to do.
And if to light on you my hap so good shall be,
I shall be glad to feed on that that would have fed on me.
And thus farewell, unkind, to whom I bent too low:
I would you wist the ship is safe that bare his sail so low.   70
Since that a lion's heart is for a wolf no prey,
With bloody mouth on simple sheep go slake your wrath, I say
With more despite and ire than I can now express,
Which to my pain though I refrain, the cause you well may
    guess:

57

As for because my self was author of this game,   75
It boots me not that, by my wrath, I should disturb the same.

24

Wyatt resteth here, that quick could never rest;
Whose heavenly gifts increasèd by disdain,
And virtue sank the deeper in his breast:
Such profit he by envy could obtain.

A head, where wisdom mysteries did frame;   5
Whose hammers beat still in that lively brain
As on a stithe, where that some work of fame
Was daily wrought to turn to Britain's gain.

A visage stern and mild; where both did grow
Vice to contemn, in virtue to rejoice;   10
Amid great storms whom grace assurèd so
To live upright and smile at fortune's choice.

A hand that taught what might be said in rhyme;
That reft Chaucer the glory of his wit;
A mark the which, unparfited for time,   15
Some may approach, but never none shall hit.

A tongue that served in foreign realms his king;
Whose courteous talk in virtue did enflame
Each noble heart; a worthy guide to bring
Our English youth by travail unto fame.   20

An eye, whose judgment none affect could blind,
Friends to allure, and foes to reconcile;
Whose piercing look did represent a mind
With virtue fraught, reposèd, void of guile.

A heart, where dread was never so impressed   25
To hide the thought that might the truth advance;
In neither fortune loft, nor yet repressed,
To swell in wealth, or yield unto mischance.

A valiant corse, where force and beauty met;
Happy, alas too happy, but for foes: 30
Livèd and ran the race that nature set;
Of manhood's shape, where she the mould did lose.

But to the heavens that simple soul is fled,
Which left with such as covet Christ to know
Witness of faith that never shall be dead;   35
Sent for our health, but not receivèd so.

Thus, for our guilt, this jewel have we lost.
The earth his bones, the heavens possess his ghost.

25
Diverse thy death do diversely bemoan.
Some, that in presence of that lively head
Lurkèd, whose breasts envy with hate had sown,
Yield Caesar's tears upon Pompeius' head.
Some, that watchèd with the murderer's knife,   5
With eager thirst to drink the guiltless blood,
Whose practice brake by happy end of life,
Weep envious tears to hear thy fame so good.
But I that know what harboured in that head,
What virtues rare were tempered in that breast,   10
Honour the place that such a jewel bred,
And kiss the ground where as thy corse doth rest
With vapoured eyes; from whence such streams avail
As Pyramus did on Thisbe's breast bewail.

59

26

The great Macedon that out of Persia chased
Darius, of whose huge power all Asia rang,
In the rich ark if Homer's rhymes he placed,
Who feignèd gests of heathen princes sang;
What holy grave, what worthy sepulture   5
To Wyatt's Psalms should Christians then purchase?
Where he doth paint the lively faith and pure,
The steadfast hope, the sweet return to grace
Of just David by perfect penitence;
Where rulers may see in a mirror clear   10
The bitter fruit of false concupiscence,
How Jewry bought Uriah's death full dear.
In Princes' hearts God's scourge yprinted deep
Might then awake out of their sinful sleep.

27

Th'Assyrians' king, in peace with foul desire
And filthy lust that stained his regal heart,
In war that should set princely hearts afire
Vanquished did yield for want of martial art.
The dent of swords from kisses seemèd strange,   5
And harder than his lady's side his targe;
From glutton feasts to soldier's fare a change;
His helmet far above a garland's charge.
Who scarce the name of manhood did retain,
Drenchèd in sloth and womanish delight,   10
Feeble of spirit, unpatient of pain,
When he had lost his honour and his right,
Proud time of wealth, in storms appalled with dread,
Murdered himself to show some manful deed.

London, hast thou accusèd me
Of breach of laws, the root of strife?
Within whose breast did boil to see
So fervent hot thy dissolute life,
That even the hate of sins, that grow   5
Within thy wicked walls so rife,
For to break forth did convert so
That terror could it not repress.
The which, by words since preachers know
What hope is left for to redress,   10
By unknown means it likèd me
My hidden burden to express,
Whereby it might appear to thee
That secret sin hath secret spite;
From justice rod no fault is free;   15
But that all such as work upright
In most quiet are next ill rest.
In secret silence of the night
This made me, with a reckless breast,
To wake thy sluggards with my bow: 20
A figure of the Lord's behest,
Whose scourge from sin the Scriptures show.
That, as the fearless thunder clap
By sudden flame at hand we know,
Of pebble stones the soundless rap   25
The dreadful plague might make thee see
Of God's wrath, that doth thee enwrap;
That pride might know, from conscience free,
How lofty works may her defend;
And envy find, as he hath sought,   30
How others seek him to offend;
And wrath taste of each cruel thought
The just shaped hire in the end;
And idle sloth, that never wrought,
To heaven his spirit lift may begin;   35

And greedy lucre live in dread
To see what hate ill got goods win;
The lechers, ye that lust do feed,
Perceive what secrecy is in sin;
And gluttons' hearts for sorrow bleed, 40
Awakened when their fault they find.
In loathsome vice each drunken wight
To stir to God, this was my mind.
Thy windows had done me no spite;
But proud people that dread no fall, 45
Clothèd with falsehood and unright,
Bred in the closures of thy wall.
But wrested to wrath in fervent zeal
Thou hear'st to strife my secret call.
Endurèd hearts no warning feel. 50
O shameless whore! Is dread then gone
By such thy foes as meant thy weal?
Oh member of false Babylon!
The shop of craft! The den of ire!
Thy dreadful doom draws fast upon. 55
Thy martyrs' blood, by sword and fire,
In heaven and earth for justice call.
The Lord shall hear their just desire;
The flame of wrath shall on thee fall;
With famine and pest lamentably 60
Stricken shall be thy lechers all;
Thy proud towers and turrets high,
Enemies to God, beat stone from stone;
Thine idols burnt that wrought iniquity;
When none thy ruin shall bemoan, 65
But render unto the right wise Lord,
That so hath judgèd Babylon,
Immortal praise with one accord.

29

Laid in my quiet bed, in study as I were,
I saw within my troubled head a heap of thoughts appear;
And every thought did show so lively in mine eyes,
That now I sighed, and then I smiled, as cause of thought did
    rise.
I saw the little boy, in thought how oft that he   5
Did wish of God to 'scape the rod, a tall young man to be;
The young man eke that feels his bones with pains oppressed,
How he would be a rich old man, to live and lie at rest;
The rich old man, that sees his end draw on so sore,
How he would be a boy again, to live so much the more.   10
Whereat full oft I smiled, to see how all these three,
From boy to man, from man to boy, would chop and change
    degree;
And musing thus, I think the case is very strange,
That man from wealth to live in woe doth ever seek to change.
Thus thoughtful as I lay I saw my withered skin,   15
How it doth show my dented jaws, the flesh was worn so
    thin.
And eke my toothless chaps, the gates of my right way
That opes and shuts as I do speak, do thus unto me say:
'Thy white and hoarish hairs, the messengers of age,
That show like lines of true belief that this life doth assuage, 20
Bid thee lay hand and feel them hanging on thy chin;
The which do write two ages past, the third now coming in.
Hang up therefore the bit of thy young wanton time,
And thou that therein beaten art, the happiest life define.'
Wereat I sighed and said, 'Farewell, my wonted joy;   25
Truss up thy pack, and trudge from me to every little boy,
And tell them thus from me, their life most happy is,
If, to their time, they reason had to know the truth of this.'

30

Martial, the things for to attain
The happy life be these, I find:
The riches left, not got with pain;
The fruitful ground; the quiet mind:
The equal friend; no grudge nor strife;   5
No charge of rule nor governance;
Without disease the healthful life;
The household of continuance;
The mean diet, no delicate fare;
Wisdom joined with simplicity;   10
The night dischargèd of all care,
Where wine may bear no sovereignty;
The chaste wife wise, without debate;
Such sleeps as may beguile the night;
Contented with thy own estate,   15
Neither wish death nor fear his might.

31

Since fortune's wrath envieth the wealth
Wherein I reignèd, by the sight
Of that that fed mine eyes by stealth
With sour, sweet, dread and delight,
Let not my grief move you to moan,   5
For I will weep and wail alone.

Sprite drave me into Boreas' reign,
Where hoary frosts the fruits do bite,
When hills were spread and every plain
With stormy winter's mantle white.   10
And yet, my dear, such was my heat,
When others freeze then did I sweat.

And now though on the sun I drive,
Whose fervent flame all things decays,
His beams in brightness may not strive   15
With light of your sweet golden rays,
Nor from my breast this heat remove
The frozen thoughts graven by love.

Nor may the waves of the salt flood
Quench that your beauty set on fire,   20
For though mine eyes forbear the food
That did relieve the hot desire,
Such as I was such will I be,
Your own: what would ye more of me?

32

When raging love with extreme pain
Most cruelly distrains my heart,
When that my tears, as floods of rain,
Bear witness of my woeful smart;
When sighs have wasted so my breath   5
That I lie at the point of death:

I call to mind the navy great
That the Greeks brought to Troia town,
And how the boisterous winds did beat
Their ships, and rent their sails adown,   10
Till Agamemnon's daughter's blood
Appeased the gods that them withstood.

And how that in those ten years' war
Full many a bloody deed was done,
And many a lord, that came full far,   15
There caught his bane, alas, too soon,
And many a good knight overrun,
Before the Greeks had Helen won.

Then think I thus: sith such repair,
So long time war of valiant men,   20
Was all to win a lady fair,
Shall I not learn to suffer then,
And think my life well spent to be
Serving a worthier wight than she?

Therefore I never will repent,   25
But pains contented still endure:
For like as when, rough winter spent,
The pleasant spring straight draweth in ure,
So after raging storms of care
Joyful at length may be my fare.   30

33

Good ladies, you that have your pleasure in exile,
Step in your foot, come take a place, and mourn with me awhile;
And such as by their lords do set but little price,
Let them sit still, it skills them not what chance comes on the dice.
But you whom love hath bound, by order of desire,   5
To love your lords, whose good deserts none other would
    require,
Come you yet once again, and set your foot by mine,
Whose woeful plight, and sorrows great, no tongue may well
    define.
My lord and love, alas, in whom consists my wealth,
Hath fortune sent to pass the seas, in hazard of his health. 10
Whom I was wont t'embrace with well contented mind
Is now amid the foaming floods, at pleasures of the wind.
There God him well preserve, and safely me him send;
Without which hope my life, alas, were shortly at an end.
Whose absence yet, although my hope doth tell me plain   15
With short return he comes anon, yet ceaseth not my pain.
The fearful dreams I have, oft times they grieve me so
That then I wake, and stand in doubt if they be true or no.

Sometime the roaring seas, me seems, they grow so high,
That my sweet lord in danger great, alas, doth often lie.   20
Another time the same doth tell me he is come,
And playing, where I shall him find, with T. his little son.
So forth I go apace to see that lifesome sight,
And with a kiss methinks I say, 'Now welcome home, my knight;
Welcome, my sweet, alas, the stay of my welfare;   25
Thy presence bringeth forth a truce betwixt me and my care.'
Then lively doth he look, and salueth me again,
And saith, 'My dear, how is it now that you have all this pain?'
Wherewith the heavy cares, that heaped are in my breast,
Break forth and me dischargeth clean of all my great unrest. 30
But when I me awake and find it but a dream,
The anguish of my former woe beginneth more extreme,
And me tormenteth so that unnethe may I find
Some hidden place to still the grief of my unquiet mind.
Thus every way you see with absence how I burn,   35
And for my wound no cure there is but hope of some return;
Save when I feel, by sour, how sweet is felt the more,
It doth abate some of my pains that I abode before.
And then unto my self I say, 'When that we two shall meet,
But little time shall seem this pain, that joy shall be so sweet'. 40
Ye winds, I ye conjure, in chiefest of your rage,
That you my lord me safely send, my sorrows to assuage;
And that I may not long abide in such excess,
Do your good will to cure a wight that liveth in distress.

34

O happy dames, that may embrace
The fruit of your delight,
Help to bewail the woeful case
And eke the heavy plight
Of me, that wonted to rejoice   5
The fortune of my pleasant choice:
Good ladies, help to fill my mourning voice.

In ship, freight with rememberance
Of thoughts and pleasures past,
He sails that hath in governance   10
My life, while it will last;
With scalding sighs, for lack of gale,
Furthering his hope, that is his sail
Toward me, the sweet port of his avail.

Alas, how oft in dreams I see   15
Those eyes, that were my food,
Which sometime so delighted me,
That yet they do me good;
Wherewith I wake with his return
Whose absent flames did make me burn.   20
But when I find the lack, Lord how I mourn.

When other lovers in arms across
Rejoice their chief delight,
Drownèd in tears to mourn my loss
I stand the bitter night   25
In my window, where I may see
Before the wind how the clouds flee.
Lo, what a mariner hath love made me!

And in green waves when the salt flood
Doth rise by rage of wind,   30
A thousand fancies in that mood
Assail my restless mind.
Alas, now drencheth my sweet foe,
That with the spoil of my heart did go,
And left me; but, alas, why did he so?   35

And when the seas wax calm again,
To chase from me annoy,
My doubtful hope doth cause me plain:
So dread cuts off my joy.

Thus is my wealth mingled with woe, 40
And of each thought a doubt doth grow:
Now he comes. Will he come? Alas, no, no.

35

The fancy which that I have servèd long
That hath alway been enemy to mine ease,
Seemèd of late to rue upon my wrong
And bade me fly the cause of my misease.
And I forthwith did press out of the throng, 5
That thought by flight my painful heart to please
Some other way, till I saw faith more strong.
And to myself I said: 'Alas, those days
In vain were spent, to run the race so long'.
And with that thought I met my guide, that plain 10
Out of the way wherein I wandered wrong
Brought me amid the hills in base Bullayn;
Where I am now, as restless to remain,
Against my will, full pleasèd with my pain.

36

Norfolk sprang thee, Lambeth holds thee dead,
Clere of the County of Cleremont though hight;
Within the womb of Ormonde's race thou bred,
And saw thy cousin crownèd in thy sight.
Shelton for love, Surrey for lord thou chase: 5
Ay me, while life did last that league was tender;
Tracing whose steps thou sawest Kelsall blaze,
Laundersey burnt, and battered Bullen render.
At Muttrell gate, hopeless of all recure,
Thine Earl half dead gave in thy hand his will; 10
Which cause did thee this pining death procure,
Ere summers four times seven thou couldst fulfill.
Ah Clere, if love had booted, care, or cost,
Heaven had not won, nor Earth so timely lost.

Last Poems

37 *Ecclesiastes, Chapter Two*

From pensive fancies then, I gan my heart revoke,
And gave me to such sporting plays as laughter might provoke,
But even such vain delights, when they most blinded me,
Always methought with smiling grace a king did ill agree.
Then sought I how to please my belly with much wine,   5
To feed me fat with costly feasts of rare delights and fine,
And other pleasures eke, to purchase me with rest,
In so great choice to find the thing that might content me best.
But, Lord, what care of mind, what sudden storms of ire,
With broken sleeps endurèd I, to compass my desire!   10
To build my houses fair then set I all my cure:
By princely acts thus strove I still to make my fame endure.
Delicious gardens eke I made to please my sight,
And graft therein all kinds of fruits that might my mouth delight.
Conduits, by lively springs, from their old course I drew   15
For to refresh the fruitful trees that in my garden grew.
Of cattle great increase I bred in little space.
Bondmen I bought, I gave them wives, and served me with
   their race.
Great heaps of shining gold by sparing gan I save,
With things of price so furnishèd as fits a prince to have.   20
To hear fair women sing sometime I did rejoice,
Ravishèd with their pleasant tunes and sweetness of their voice.
Lemans I had, so fair and of so lively hue
That who so gazèd in their face might well their beauty rue.
Never erst sat there king so rich in David's seat: 25
Yet still methought for so small gain the travail was too great.
From my desirous eyes I hid no pleasant sight,
Nor from my heart no kind of mirth that might give them delight;
Which was the only fruit I reaped of all my pain:
To feed my eyes and to rejoice my heart with all my gain.   30

But when I made my compt, with how great care of mind
And heart's unrest that I had sought so wasteful fruit to find,
Then was I stricken straight with that abusèd fier,
To glory in that goodly wit that compassed my desire.
But fresh before my eyes grace did my faults renew: 35
What gentle callings I had fled, my ruin to pursue,
What raging pleasures past, peril and hard escape,
What fancies in my head had wrought the liquor of the grape.
The error then I saw that their frail hearts doth move,
Which strive in vain for to compare with him that sits above;   40
In whose most perfect works such craft appeareth plain
That to the least of them there may no mortal hand attain.
And like as lightsome day doth shine above the night,
So dark to me did folly seem, and wisdom's beams as bright.
Whose eyes did seem so clear, motes to discern and find;   45
But will had closèd folly's eyes which gropèd like the blind.
Yet death and time consume all wit and worldly fame,
And look what end that folly hath, and wisdom hath the same.
Then said I thus: Oh Lord, may not thy wisdom cure
The wailful wrongs and hard conflicts that folly doth endure?   50
To sharp my wits so fine then why took I this pain?
Now find I well this noble search may eke be callèd vain.
As slander's loathsome bruit sounds folly's just reward,
Is put to silence all by time, and brought in small regard;
Even so doth time devour the noble blast of fame,   55
Which should resound their glories great that do deserve the
    same.
Thus present changes chase away the wonders past,
Nor is the wise man's fatal thread yet longer spun to last.
Then in this wretchèd vale of life I loathèd plain
When I beheld our fruitless pains to compass pleasures vain.   60
My travail this avail hath me producèd, lo!
An heir unknown shall reap the fruit that I in seed did sow.
But whereunto the Lord his nature shall incline
Who can foreknow, into whose hands I must my goods resign?
But, Lord, how pleasant sweet then seemed the idle life,   65

That never chargèd was with care, nor burdenèd with strife;
And vile the greedy trade of them that toil so sore
To leave to such their travail's fruit that never sweat therefore.
What is that pleasant gain, which is that sweet relief,
That should delay the bitter taste that we feel of our grief?   70
The gladsome days we pass to search a simple gain,
The quiet nights, with broken sleeps, to feed a restless brain.
What hope is left us then, what comfort doth remain?
Our quiet hearts for to rejoice with the fruits of our pain.
If that be true, who may himself so happy call   75
As I, whose free and sumptuous expense doth shine beyond
    them all.
Surely it is a gift and favour of the Lord
Liberally to spend our goods, the ground of all discord;
And wretched hearts have they that let their treasures mould,
And carry the rod that scourgeth them that glory in their gold. 80
But I do know by proof, whose riches bear such bruit,
What stable wealth may stand in waste by heaping of such fruit.

38 *Ecclesiastes, Chapter Three*

Like to the steerless boat that swerves with every wind,
The slipper top of worldly wealth by cruel proof I find.
Scarce hath the seed, whereof that nature formeth man,
Receivèd life, when death him yields to earth where he began.
The grafted plants with pain, whereof we hopèd fruit,   5
To root them up, with blossoms spread, then is our chief pursuit.
That erst we rearèd up we undermine again,
And shred the sprays whose growth sometime we labourèd
    with pain.
Each froward threatening cheer of fortune makes us plain,
And every pleasant show revives our woeful hearts again.   10
Ancient walls to raze is our unstable guise,
And of their weatherbeaten stones to build some new device.
New fancies daily spring, which fade returning moe;

And now we practice to obtain that straight we must forgo.
Sometime we seek to spare that afterward we waste,　　　15
And that we travailed sore to knit for to unclose as fast.
In sober silence now our quiet lips we close,
And with unbridled tongues forthwith our secret hearts
　　disclose.
Such as in folded arms we did embrace, we hate;
Whom straight we reconcile again and banish all debate.　　20
My seed with labour sown such fruit produceth me
To waste my life in contraries that never shall agree.
From God these heavy cares are sent for our unrests,
And with such burdens for our wealth he fraughteth full our
　　breasts.
All that the Lord hath wrought hath beauty and good grace,　25
And to each thing assignèd is the proper time and place.
And granted eke to man, of all the world's estate
And of each thing wrought in the same, to argue and debate.
Which art, though it approach the heavenly knowledge most,
To search the natural ground of things, yet all is labour lost.　30
But then the wandering eyes, that long for surety sought,
Found that by pain no certain wealth might in this world be
　　bought.
Who liveth in delight and seeks no greedy thrift,
But freely spends his goods, may think it as a secret gift.
Fulfillèd shall it be, what so the Lord intend,　　　35
Which no device of man's wit may advance, nor yet defend;
Who made all thing of nought, that Adam's children might
Learn how to dread the Lord, that wrought such wonders in
　　their sight.
The grisly wonders past, which time wears out of mind,
To be renewèd in our days the Lord hath so assigned.　　40
Lo, thus his careful scourge doth steal on us unware,
Which, when the flesh hath clean forgot, he doth again repair.
When I in this vain search had wandered sore my wit,
I saw a royal throne where as that Justice should have sit;
Instead of whom I saw, with fierce and cruel mood,　　45

73

Where Wrong was set, that bloody beast, that drunk the
  guiltless' blood.
Then thought I thus: One day the Lord shall sit in doom,
To view his flock and choose the pure: the spotted have no room.
Ye be such scourges sent that each aggrievèd mind,
Like the brute beasts that swell in rage and fury by their kind,   50
His error may confess, when he hath wrestled long;
And then with patience may him arm, the sure defence of
    wrong.
For death, that of the beast the carrion may devour,
Unto the noble kind of man presents the fatal hour.
The perfect form that God hath either given to man   55
Or other beast, dissolve it shall to earth where it began.
And who can tell if that the soul of man ascend,
Or with the body if it die, and to the ground descend?
Whereof each greedy heart that riches seeks to gain,
Gather may he that savoury fruit that springeth of his pain.   60
A mean convenient wealth I mean to take in worth,
And with a hand of largess eke in measure pour it forth.
For treasures spent in life the body doth sustain;
The heir shall waste the hoarded gold amassèd with much pain.
Nor may foresight of man such order give in life   65
For to foreknow who shall rejoice their gotten good with strife.

39

When reckless youth in quiet breast,
Set on by wrath, revenge and cruelty,
After long war patience had oppressed,
And justice wrought by princely equity;
My Denny, then mine error, deep impressed   5
Began to work despair of liberty,
Had not David, the perfect warrior, taught
That of my fault thus pardon should be sought.

74

Oh Lord, upon whose will dependeth my welfare,
To call upon thy holy name since day nor night I spare,
Grant that the just request of this repentant mind
So pierce thine ears that in thy sight some favour it may find.
My soul is fraughted full with grief of follies past;   5
My restless body doth consume and death approacheth fast;
Like them whose fatal thread thy hand hath cut in twain,
Of whom there is no further bruit, which in their graves remain.
Oh Lord, thou hast cast me headlong to please my foe,
Into a pit all bottomless, where as I plain my woe.   10
The burden of thy wrath it doth me sore oppress,
And sundry storms thou hast me sent of terror and distress.
The faithful friends are fled and banished from my sight,
And such as I have held full dear have set my friendship light.
My durance doth persuade of freedom such despair   15
That, by the tears that bain my breast, mine eyesight doth appair.
Yet did I never cease thine aid for to desire,
With humble heart and stretchèd hands for to appease thy ire.
Wherefore dost thou forbear, in the defence of thine,
To show such tokens of thy power, in sight of Adam's line,   20
Whereby each feeble heart with faith might so be fed
That in the mouth of thy elect thy mercies might be spread?
The flesh that feedeth worms can not thy love declare,
Nor such set forth thy faith as dwell in the land of despair.
In blind endurèd hearts light of thy lively name   25
Cannot appear, as cannot judge the brightness of the same.
Nor blazèd may thy name be by the mouth of those
Whom death has shut in silence, so as they may not disclose.
The lively voice of them that in thy word delight
Must be the trump that must resound the glory of thy might.   30
Wherefore I shall not cease, in chief of my distress,
To call on thee till that the sleep my wearied limbs oppress.
And in the morning eke, when that the sleep is fled,
With floods of salt repentant tears to wash my restless bed.

Within this careful mind, burdened with care and grief,   35
Why dost thou not appear, Oh Lord, that shouldst be his relief?
My wretched state behold, whom death shall straight assail;
Of one from youth afflicted still, that never did but wail.
The dread, lo, of thine ire hath trod me under feet;
The scourges of thine angry hand hath made death seem full
      sweet.   40
Like to the roaring waves the sunken ship surround,
Great heaps of care did swallow me and I no succour found.
For they whom no mischance could from my love divide
Are forcèd, for my greater grief, from me their face to hide.

41
The sudden storms that heave me to and fro
Had well near piercèd faith, my guiding sail;
For I, that on the noble voyage go
To succour truth, and falsehood to assail,
Constrainèd am to bear my sails full low   5
And never could attain some pleasant gale;
For unto such the prosperous winds do blow
As run from port to port to seek avail.
This bred despair, whereof such doubts did grow
That I gan faint, and all my courage fail.   10
But now, my Blage, mine error well I see:
Such goodly light King David giveth me.

42 *Psalm Seventy Three*

Though, Lord, to Israel thy graces plenteous be;
I mean to such with pure intent as fix their trust in thee;
Yet whiles the faith did faint that should have been my guide,
Like them that walk in slipper paths my feet began to slide,
Whiles I did grudge at those that glory in their gold,   5
Whose loathsome pride rejoiceth wealth, in quiet as they would.

To see by course of years what nature doth appair,
The palaces of princely form succeed from heir to heir;
From all such travails free as 'long to Adam's seed;
Neither withdrawn from wicked words by danger nor by
    dread   10
Whereof their scornful pride; and gloried with their eyes,
As garments clothe the naked man, so are they clad in vice.
Thus as they wish succeeds the mischief that they mean,
Whose glutton cheeks sloth feeds so fat as scant their eyes be
    seen.
Unto whose cruel power most men for dread are fain   15
To bend and bow with lofty looks, whiles they vaunt in their
    reign
And in their bloody hands, whose cruelty doth frame
The wailful works that scourge the poor without regard of
    blame.
To tempt the living God they think it no offence,
And pierce the simple with their tongues that can make no
    defence.   20
Such proofs before the just, to cause the hearts to waver,
Be set like cups mingled with gall, of bitter taste and savour.
Then say thy foes in scorn, that taste no other food,
But suck the flesh of thy elect and bathe them in their blood:
'Should we believe the Lord doth know and suffer this?   25
Foolèd be he with fables vain that so abusèd is.'
In terror of the just thus reigns iniquity,
Armèd with power, laden with gold, and dread for cruelty.
Then vain the war might seem that I by faith maintain
Against the flesh, whose false effects my pure heart would
    distain.   30
For I am scourgèd still, that no offence have done,
By wrath's children; and from my birth my chastising begun.
When I beheld their pride and slackness of thy hand,
I gan bewail the woeful state wherein thy chosen stand.
And as I sought whereof thy sufferance, Lord, should grow, 35
I found no wit could pierce so far, thy holy dooms to know,

And that no mysteries nor doubt could be mistrust
Till I come to the holy place, the mansion of the just,
Where I shall see what end thy justice shall prepare
For such as build on worldly wealth, and dye their colours
    fair.   40
Oh, how their ground is false and all their building vain!
And they shall fall, their power shall fail that did their pride
    maintain.
As chargèd hearts with care, that dream some pleasant turn,
After their sleep find their abuse, and to their plaint return,
So shall their glory fade; thy sword of vengeance shall   45
Unto their drunken eyes, in blood, disclose their errors all.
And when their golden fleece is from their back yshorn,
The spots that underneath were hid thy chosen sheep shall
    scorn.
And till that happy day my heart shall swell in care,
My eyes yield tears, my years consume between hope and
    despair.   50
Lo, how my spirits are dull, and all thy judgements dark;
No mortal head may scale so high, but wonder at thy work.
Alas, how oft my foes have framèd my decay;
But when I stood in dread to drench, thy hands did still me stay.
And in each voyage that I took to conquer sin,   55
Thou wert my guide, and gave me grace to comfort me therein.
And when my withered skin unto my bones did cleave,
And flesh did waste, thy grace did then my simple spirits relieve.
In other succour then, Oh Lord, why should I trust,
But only thine, whom I have found in thy behight so just.   60
And for such dread or gain, as shall thy name refuse,
Shall perish with their golden gods that did their hearts seduce.
Where I, that in thy word have set my trust and joy,
The high reward that 'longs thereto shall quietly enjoy.
And my unworthy lips, inspired with thy grace,   65
Shall thus forespeak thy secret works in sight of Adam's race.

Give ear to my suit, Lord, fromward hide not thy face.
Behold, hearking in grief, lamenting how I pray.
My foes they bray so loud, and eke threap on so fast,
Buckled to do me scathe, so is their malice bent.
Care pierceth my entrails and travaileth my sprite;   5
The grisly fear of death environeth my breast;
A trembling cold of dread clean overwhelmeth my heart.
'O,' think I, 'had I wings like to the simple dove,
This peril might I fly, and seek some place of rest
In wilder woods, where I might dwell far from these cares.'   10
What speedy way of wing my plaints should they lay on
To 'scape the stormy blast that threatened is to me!
Rein those unbridled tongues! Break that conjurèd league!
For I deciphered have amid our town the strife:
Guile and wrong keep the walls, they ward both day and
       night;   15
And while mischief with care doth keep the marketstede;
Whilst wickedness with craft in heaps swarm through the street.
Ne my declarèd foe wrought me all this reproach;
By harm so looked for, it weigheth half the less.
For though mine enemy's hap had been for to prevail,   20
I could have hid my face from venom of his eye.
It was a friendly foe, by shadow of goodwill,
Mine old fere and dear friend, my guide, that trappèd me:
Where I was wont to fetch the cure of all my care,
And in his bosom hid my secret zeal to God.   25
Such sudden surprise quick may them hell devour,
Whilst I invoke the Lord, whose power shall me defend.
My prayer shall not cease from that the sun ascends
Till he his haulture win and hides him in the sea.
With words of hot effect, that moveth from heart contrite,   30
Such humble suit, O Lord, doth pierce thy patient ear.
It was the Lord that brake the bloody compacts of those
That prelooked on with ire to slaughter me and mine.

The everlasting God whose kingdom hath no end,
Whom, by no tale to dread he could divert from sin,   35
The conscience unquiet he strikes with heavy hand,
And proves their force in faith whom he swore to defend.
Butter falls not so soft as doth his patience long,
And overpasseth fine oil running not half so smooth.
But when his sufferance finds that bridled wrath provokes,   40
He threateneth wrath, he whets more sharp than any tool can
    file.
Friar, whose harm and tongue presents the wicked sort
Of those false wolves, with coats that do their ravin hide,
That swear to me by heaven, the footstool of the Lord,
Who though force had hurt my fame, they did not touch my
    life: 45
Such patching care I loathe as feeds the wealth with lies.
But in th'other Psalm of David find I ease:
Iacta curam tuam super dominum et ipse te enutriet.

44

The storms are past, these clouds are overblown,
And humble cheer great rigour hath repressed.
For the default is set a pain foreknown,
And patience graft in a determined breast.
And in the heart where heaps of grief were grown   5
The sweet revenge hath planted mirth and rest;
No company so pleasant as mine own.
....
Thraldom at large hath made this prison free;
Danger well past, remembered, works delight.   10
Of lingering doubts such hope is sprung pardie,
That nought I find displeasant in my sight,
But when my glass presenteth unto me
The cureless wound that bleedeth day and night,
To think, alas, such hap should granted be   15
Unto a wretch that hath no heart to fight,

To spill that blood that hath so oft been shed
For Britain's sake, alas, and now is dead.

Notes

Virgil's Aeneid

Probably written about 1537-8, perhaps a little later. As the first blank verse written in English its historical importance can hardly be exaggerated. There has been some debate about his indebtedness to Italian translations of Virgil in unrhymed verse, but although he would have known about *versi sciolti* it is unlikely that he used it as a model. The influence of Gavin Douglas is easier to point to, for one can see it affecting some of Surrey's vocabulary choices. Douglas's *Aeneid* was complete in 1513 and, although not published until 1553, circulated in manuscript. Surrey had probably possessed a copy since boyhood, and remembered it in the way one retains a Latin crib. However, he has attempted a stylistic approximation to the Latin quite unlike anything in Douglas, who was mainly concerned with getting the whole meaning of the original across (Book II, for example, is 804 lines in Virgil, 1068 in Surrey, and 1462 in Douglas). Although Surrey's version varies in quality, my reason for giving only two-fifths of it here was one of space, so that the Virgil translations should not overshadow the other poems. At its best Surrey's Virgil is magnificent, the bare, classical power of the long speeches being more like Racine than anything else in English literature. In this poem we can see the nature of English poetry being transformed in one of the great moments of our history.

1

1 *whisted* become silent   *attent* attentive   10 *Dolopes* Dolopian   *Ulysses' wagèd soldiar* mercenary of Ulysses. 'Soldiar' is three syllables, hence old spelling retained. 15 Surrey sometimes has Troy as one syllable and sometimes as two ('Troye'). I have followed Nott's practice of making this 'Troia'. 17 *plaint eschews* grief wishes to avoid   21 *high* is a misreading of Douglas's 'in hy' (meaning 'in haste').   25 *so*

wandered it at point was sufficiently well known 35 *fet*
reached 36 *discharged* gave vent to *dole* grief 40
pight pitched camp 42 *scatheful* harmful 52 *caves*
hollow insides *uncouth* unknown 54 *rout* crowd
62 *annoy* damage 71 *blind forecast* lack of forethought
2
298 *gin* contrivance 300 *children* boys *maids* girls
303 *subtil* cleverly contrived 307 *harness* armour 312
leeved believed 313 *Disclosèd eft* opened again 315
of fest festive 324 i.e., during the moon's first quarter
when it gives no light. 326 Sinon was the man left behind
by the Greeks who persuaded the Trojans to take the horse
within their walls. 339 *conjurèd* conspiratorial 346
bowln swollen 371 i.e., enough has been done for the
kingdom of Priam 375 *privy* household 383 *resounèd*
resounded 392 *silly* simple, rustic *astonied* amazed
396 *flash* small bursts of flame 402 *feres* comrades 403
brent burned 403 *in press* in haste
3
971 *sheen* shining 980 *sith* since then 989 *wood* mad
1002 *ugsome* hideous, gruesome 1021 *clepes* shouts
1027 *Abashèd* confounded *woxe* waxed 1041 *make*
mate 1054 *accoll* embrace 1055 *image* is stressed on
the second syllable as in French. 1065 *lusty* pleasant. Perhaps
this should be emended to 'lofty'.
4
2 *playe* wound 10 *pole* sky
18 i.e., cowardice indicates a heart deviated from its true
nature. Surrey's desire to reproduce the terseness of the Latin
(*degeneres animos timor arguit*) occasionally results in obscurity,
as can also be seen in line 36.
20 *achievèd* had a more positive meaning than it has nowadays
of performed successfully with honour (although some of our
literary criticism seems to retain the medieval, chivalric use of
this word).
24 *genial brands* nuptial torches

26 Sychaeus, her husband, was murdered by her brother, Pygmalion. So Pygmalion is the slaughterer and not the one slaughtered.

38 *Bainèd* bathed   40 *plaint* lamentation   *spill* waste
43 *dole* mourning, grief

46-7 i.e., whom the soil of Africa, rich in triumphant honours, breeds. This reversed order is quite common in Surrey, as in 'the kindled mind with love' (69) and 'stricken hind with shaft' (88).

56 *what shall* why should   58 *purveyance* providence

67-8 The metre becomes awkward in modern spelling. *Watery* is two syllables; *Orion* is stressed on the first syllable; *ships* is 'shippes' (two syllables). There is more stress on the '-ly' of *unfriendly* than there would be in modern English.

72 *hogrels* young sheep

75 *marriage* is trisyllabic. French-style pronunciation still occurs in Surrey, but on nothing like the scale of earlier writers.

79 *fat* rich   91 *thirling* piercing   92 *lands* glades

5

Aeneas has just been visited by Mercury who urged his departure.

360 *bestraught* distraught   375 *address* get ready   387 *avail* set sail by ebb tide   388 *bestead* served by   390 *Thyas* has been misread by Surrey as someone's name. Virgil's 'Thyias' means a 'Thyad' (i.e., a Bacchanal).   394 'Dauncing' stressed on second syllable, hence old spelling.   412 *do away this mind* discard this idea, change your mind   413 *tyrans* ruler. Stress on second syllable.   450 *advise* order   461 *advise* makes recall   466 *either head* means either that of Jove or Mercury   476 *braid* suddenly cry out   481 *what* why   *cheer* looks   482 *me reserve* restrain myself   489 *fonded* foolishly enamoured   492 *drive* driven on   508 *abye* pay   509 *bruit* rumour, news   517 *tapets* coverlets

6

789 *prest* quickly   791 *warp* be towed   796 *Then it behove* you should have behaved like that then   801 *drenchèd*

drowned   *feres* companions   804 *debate* strife   809
nation is French-style three syllables, as in line 825   815 *wreaker*
avenger. The stress seems to be on the second syllable here,
whereas in line 837 it is on the first.   821 *of force* of necessity
831 *brook* enjoy   835 *cinders* ashes   843 *fordo* destroy
850 The body is her own body (i.e., Anne's). 854 *mind* intention
865 *clamb* climbed   868 *weed* clothing   869 *study*
contemplation   879 *unwroken* unavenged

From the Italian

Surrey's interest in Petrarch now looks much like his interest
in Virgil, as a poet who possessed the classical virtues of
balance, symmetry, chaste diction and elegance; stylistic
aspects in which English poetry and the English language itself
were felt to be lacking. These translations, therefore, are more
like adaptations than actual translations, as Surrey's aim was
to fit Petrarchan style on to an English reality, which can be
seen in sonnets which are not translations (27 and 28, for
example) but are still dominated by Petrarchan, neo-classical
ideas of style.

7

This poem is a fine illustration of the above remarks, for
although it is a translation of a sonnet by Petrarch (*Zefiro torna,
e 'l bel tempo rima*), the old-fashioned nature of some of its
language and its use of traditional imagery makes it read as
an act of homage to medieval English poetry, and not as any
attempt to introduce a foreign sensibility into the language.
1 *soote* sweet   5 *springs* put forth new growth   6 *pale*
fence (that around a deer park).   8 *flete* float, swim   11
mings 'produces by mixing' (OED)   12 *bale* harm

8

From Petrarch's sonnet, *Pommi ove 'l sole occide i fiori e l'erba*;
which is itself based on Horace, Odes I, 22.
4 *sad* serious
6 This seems an inadequate contrast, and it is not in Petrarch.

Either the line is corrupt, or Surrey misread the Italian, or the demands of the pentameter may have imposed the tautology upon him.

9

From Petrarch's sonnet, *Amor, che nel penser mio vive e regna*; which has also been translated by Wyatt as 'The long love that in my thought doth harbour'. An analysis of the complexity of this poem can be found in Alistair Fowler, *Conceitful Thought, the Interpretation of English Renaissance Poems* (Edinburgh, 1975), pp.21-5.

4 i.e., my face often shows I am in love with her.

5-8 i.e., she, however, who has taught me to endure the pain of love, and to conceal any expression of it, no matter how intense my feelings may be, by the use of modest looks, is immediately made angry by such manifestations.

11 *my lord*   love

10

This seems to be a version of Ariosto, *Orlando Furioso*, I, 78-85.

11

From Petrarch, *Lassare il velo o per sole o per ombra.*

12

From Petrarch, *Or che 'l ciel e la terra e 'l vento tace*; which is based on the famous night passage in the *Aeneid*, Book IV.

4 The stars are the subject of this sentence. There are other instances in Surrey of plural subjects having singular verbs.

13

There is no known source for this very Petrarchan sonnet.

6 *lively dooms*   'persons of quick and lively judgment' (Nott).

14

This has been put in stanza form, instead of the usual printing as one continuous verse paragraph, because the rhyme scheme is *terza rima*, and the poem makes better rhythmic and poetic sense if that structure is stressed. It draws on various passages from Petrarch.

2 *lustiness* gaiety, beauty   14 *reduceth* brings back   32 *haunted* frequented   33 *chance* fortune befallen one

36 *lace*   net, snare   49 *plain*   lament

15

George Gascoine in his *Certain Notes...* (1575) speaks of 'the commonest sort of verse which we use nowadays (viz. the long verse of twelve and fourteen syllables) I know not certainly how to name it, unless I should say that it doth consist of poulter's measure, which giveth twelve for one dozen and fourteen for another.' It was Surrey's success with this verse-form which made it so popular in the 1560s and 1570s, although hardly anybody has had a good word for it since then. Most of such verses were probably written to be sung, and it seems to have appealed to Surrey because it allowed him to sustain a relatively lengthy narrative or logical argument in musical form. If one reads it slowly, resisting the obvious rhythmic pull of the verse, it can have a certain attraction, which a jog trot and scamper through it will not provide. The opening lines of this poem are based on Ariosto, the rest on Petrarch.

8 *aim* hazard   13 *lets* prevents   14 *spilt* wasted
17 *lusts* wishes: i.e., I know how to make my will conform to the wishes of others. 24 *The hammer of the restless forge*   the workings of the mind   30 *resolving all his fume*   to end all his pain

40 'Heraldic writers say, that the lion is of so courageous a nature, that no compulsion or beating can make him couch; but that he is so gentle-hearted, that if he see a whelp beaten he will immediately become couchant, as if interceding to have the chastisement remitted' (Nott). The lion was an heraldic beast of the Howards.

42 *lese* lose   43 *yielded* (yelden) submissive   47 *trains* allurements

Poems

16

Perhaps one of Surrey's earliest poems, written around the age of seventeen. It was praised by Warton for 'possessing

88

almost the ease and gallantry of Waller'.
17
The Duke of Richmond died of consumption on 22 July 1536. According to his father, Surrey remained heartbroken for a year. On 3 October 1536 the rebellion known as the 'Pilgrimage of Grace' broke out in Lincolnshire, demanding reforms (return of power to the nobility, suppression of upstarts like Cromwell, return to the old religion) with which Norfolk and Surrey might well have been in sympathy. Norfolk was sent to put down the rising, which was soon done, but a more serious outbreak occurred in Yorkshire; thus Surrey went to join his father and spent a winter in the north.

When, in the next year, Sir Edward Seymour accused him of having sympathized with the rebels, Surrey struck him; an action which took place at court (in the park at Hampton), so it was theoretically punishable by the loss of the offending arm; although Surrey was, in fact, only confined to Windsor Castle for a few weeks.

4 *Ver* spring   5 *the wedded birds so late*   the recently wedded birds (traditionally assumed to marry on St Valentine's Day) 7 *hateless short debate*   friendly emulation in the martial arts 8 *rakehell*   madcap, careless   14 *bent* inclined
18
See previous poem. Courthope writes: 'I know of few verses in the whole range of human poetry in which the voice of nature utters the accents of grief with more simplicity and truth; it seems to me to be the most pathetic *personal* elegy in English poetry.'

3 *childish* of my youth (not childhood)   7 *maidens' tower*: 'that part of the castle where the court ladies had their apartments' (Nott).   9 *sales* chambers   11 Tigers were symbols of unfeeling cruelty   13 *palm play*   *jeu de pâume* (a form of tennis)   16 *bait* attract. The leads must either be the battlements from which the ladies looked down on the game (assuming it was played in the open), or the galleries of a 'real tennis' court.   17 The lists for jousting were strewn with gravel.

A mistress's favour was tied about the helmet.   29 *holts*
woods   30 *availed* slack   32 *'Chasse à forcer* is the old
hunting term for that game which is run down, in opposition
to the *chasse à tirer* which is shot' (Nott).   42 *berain* rain
down   44 *Upsuppèd* all consumed, supped up   51
freedom has both meanings of *'chivalry'* and *'freedom'*.

19

Surrey's relationship with 'Geraldine', and her relationship to
his poems, are still matters for speculation. The fantastic nature
of the account given by Nashe in his *Unfortunate Traveller*,
whereby all the love poems were written for her and Surrey
entered the lists at Florence as her champion against all comers,
has led to its rejection, since it is clear Surrey never went to
Italy; and it is also claimed that this sonnet was written in 1537
when she was only nine years old. However, that will not
dispose of Geraldine, even if one believes (as I do not) that a
man of twenty cannot fall in love with a girl of nine. If one
puts the first meeting in 1541 (as Nott does) when she was
thirteen (in the courtly tradition a girl became eligible for love
addresses at the age of twelve) and Surrey twenty-four, there
is nothing suspicious about an affair of that kind.

The known facts about her are these. She was Lady Elizabeth
Fitzgerald (Fitzgeralds were also known as Geraldines or
Garretts). Her grandfather was the ninth Earl of Kildare. She
was born in Ireland in 1528, came to England in 1533, and was
in the service of Princess Elizabeth in 1539, entering that of
Queen Catherine Howard in 1540. She married Sir Antony
Browne, Master of the Horse, in December 1542. He was sixty
years old at the time and she was fourteen.

Besides this poem there are others (36, for example) which
are hard to make sense of unless one sees them as addressed
to her, so the relationship should be taken seriously. Naturally
it was of the courtly kind and there is no reason to believe that
adultery took place between them. He was her knight and she
accepted his service in strict accordance with the courtly code.

1 *Tuscan* (Tuscane) Tuscany   2 The Fitzgeralds were

descended from the Geraldi of Florence.   3 *The western isle* Ireland   *Cambria* Wales   6 Her mother was a first cousin to Henry VIII   8 *ghostly food* spiritual nourishment 9-11 The households of Princesses Mary and Elizabeth moved about a good deal, and would have stopped on a number of occasions at Hunsden and Hampton, on any of which Surrey could have met her. Hunsden, in Norfolk, belonged to Surrey's father until he became Duke of Norfolk in 1542. Surrey was born and spent much of his early childhood, until the age of seven, there.
13 i.e., her beauty is a matter of heredity, her virtues are a gift from heaven.

20
3 i.e., or if I did not mind sullying.   6 *wite* blame; i.e., I could well be accused of wilfulness.   8 The falcon was the most generous of birds, the kite the most ravenous.   11 *pease* pea (normal singular form at time)   18 *brittle* inconstant, fickle. Nott comments: 'The harbour where the bottom is not firm enough to hold the anchor.'   23 *ure* action, practice; something actually happening.   30 *gander's foe* fox. Fox-hunting was considered a vulgar sport at the time, in contrast to the royal sport of deer-hunting.   43 *lese* lose.

21
13 *Iwis* indeed   21 *wrasteth new her grace* artificially changes the expression on her face into a pleasant one   27 i.e., I am simply one in a queue of lovers.

22
This is a reply to the previous poem. Surrey has written elsewhere in the guise of a woman (33 and 34). The poem provides fairly strong evidence that Surrey did at least write some of his poems to Geraldine, for the poem has caught very well the pert, Alice-in-Wonderland tone of voice which a clever girl around the age of ten or twelve has, with the slyness of the 'crafty cloak' (a child's idea of wit) and the juvenile learning laboriously displayed in the reference to the Old Testament (no longer in our Bible although it was in the Vulgate).

26 *in worth* patiently   28 *Child* probably means 'knight' here   37 *let them of their lust* prevent them getting their own way.

23

Tottel gives this the title, 'A song written by the Earl of Surrey to a lady that refused to dance with him'. The lady has been identified as Anne Stanhope, wife of Sir Edward Seymour. The Stanhope family had two wolves supporting their escutcheon. With the execution of Catherine Howard in February 1542 the position of the Howards had become precarious again, and overtures of friendship were made towards the Seymours as they had been in 1538. At some such function Surrey, still loath to form any alliance with these upstarts, must have had his advances rejected by Lady Hertford (Anne Stanhope). This, and the previous two poems, should show that Surrey was perfectly capable of a certain self-mocking, objective understanding of himself.

1 *fere* companion   2 The lion was an heraldic emblem of the Howard family. Surrey is describing himself.   11 *froward* unfriendly   *grace* attitude. Anne Stanhope was renowned for her high spirits, pride, and arrogance.   13 *beck* nod 14 *unmeet* unworthy

30 Thomas Howard, Surrey's grandfather, second Duke of Norfolk, commanded the English army which annihilated the Scots at Flodden Field in 1513, and so he overthrew James IV of Scotland.

35-40 Lord Thomas Howard, half-brother of Surrey's father, secretly married in 1536 Lady Margaret Douglas, daughter of Henry VIII's sister, Margaret. Since both the Princesses Mary and Elizabeth had been declared illegitimate by Act of Parliament, she was thus the nearest heir to the throne. Henry VIII was furious at a marriage which had not only been performed without his permission but was politically dangerous, and Lord Thomas Howard was thrown into the Tower on 18 July 1536, for high treason. Lady Margaret was also confined there (apart from her husband) until he died in October 1537.

41 *Other* Lady Margaret, but could be plural   46 *trace*
pursue
24

Wyatt died on 11 October 1542, at a time when Surrey had probably just emerged from prison where he had spent sixteen days for issuing a challenge to a courtier called John à Leigh. By August 1542 France and Spain were at open war with each other, and this left Henry VIII free to attack Scotland; so this projected invasion was probably the reason why Surrey was so quickly released, since his military talents were required in the north. On October 21 Norfolk and Surrey entered Scotland at the head of 20,000 men. They met little resistance, and pillaged and burned as they went (including the razing of Kelsall, see poem 36), but had to withdraw after only nine days, for lack of provisions.

How well Surrey knew Wyatt (or even if he knew him at all) it is impossible to say with certainty. Since Wyatt was a protegé of Cromwell he should, in theory, have been a member of the enemy, Protestant camp, although the question of Surrey's religious beliefs is a complex one (see note to poem 28). With Cromwell's downfall in 1540, Wyatt too was arrested for treason early in 1541. He was pardoned later that year on the intercession of Queen Catherine, who was herself persuaded by Surrey and his sister. The obvious respect and affection shown by Surrey in this and the following poem makes Padelford's claim that the two became friends at this time, and remained so until Wyatt's death, seem reasonable. It is an undoubted fact that Wyatt's son was on very close terms with Surrey, for he was one of those involved in the scandalous events of 19 January 1543 (see poem 28).

7 *stithe* anvil   15 i.e., unperfected for lack of time   21 *none affect* no passion   27-8 'Neither so elevated by good, nor so depressed by bad fortune, as to be puffed up by prosperity, or to sink under affliction' (Nott).   29 *corse* body, frame   35 A reference to Wyatt's paraphrases of the Penitential Psalms.

25

14 One should bear in mind that this was written before Shakespeare had turned the story into one of the world's great jokes.

26

1 Stress on first syllable of Macedon. This is Alexander the Great who is said to have carried his copy of Homer in a valuable casket which was one of the spoils of the victory over Darius.
4 *gests* exploits   6 Stress on second syllable of *purchase*
The end of this poem seems a fairly overt reference to Henry VIII, which makes one feel the subject of the next poem is the same monarch.

27

Sardanapalus lived (according to Ctesias' *Persica*) in great luxury. He was besieged in Nineveh by the Medes for two years, then set fire to his palace, burning himself and his whole court to death. Jones points out that he was commonly cited as an example of degenerate kingship, and gives examples from Gower and Lydgate.
8 *charge* weight

28

On 19 January 1543 Surrey and a party of young men, including Thomas Clere and Thomas Wyatt the younger, had dinner in a tavern in Cheapside, left around nine o'clock, and went down towards the river carrying 'stone bows' (catapults used for shooting rabbits and birds). They broke a few windows of city merchants' houses on the way, then hired wherries to take them down river to the left bank, where women of the town and their pimps gathered, and fired a few puritanical shots at them. Surrey was summoned to appear before the Privy Council on April 1, where he was accused of eating meat during Lent and 'breaking with stone bows of certain windows'. He pleaded alleviating circumstances as far as the meat eating was concerned, but 'touching the stone bows, he could not deny but he had done very evil therein'. He was committed to the Fleet prison, along with Wyatt and another, and seems to have been freed by the end of May.

These remarkable antics have led to a widespread assumption that the poem is an exercise in the mock heroic which gives expression to a Protestant ethic for which Surrey, 'born the heir apparent of the foremost exponent of the ancient hereditary rights, privileges, and prerogatives of England's peers and the papacy' (Casady, *op.cit.* 7), could only have felt contempt. Padelford refers to it as 'this inimitable mock heroic poem' and says that 'it may have been during his confinement that this irrepressible young nobleman composed this waggish satire'. The dating seems right, but whether it can be called a 'waggish satire' has been questioned by H.A. Mason (*Humanism and Poetry in the Early Tudor Period*, (1959), 243-5) who calls the poem a serious expression of Protestant sentiments. What evidence we have (the opinion of the Spanish Ambassador, for example, who was convinced Surrey was infected with Lutheranism) suggests that he probably was more radical in religious matters than someone of the 'Protestant party' like Hertford. The fact that Surrey sympathized with such beliefs, however, does not have to make this poem a serious statement of them. If one sets the poem in its background of the year 1542, with Surrey's imprisonment, the campaign in Scotland which Surrey seems to have hated ('Spite drove me into Boreas' reign'), and the marriage of Geraldine in December, one has an almost perfect recipe for an outburst of frustration in radical ideas and actions. An intelligent man who holds radical beliefs and is induced by drink, like-minded companions, and a general sense of life not going well, to direct that discontent at the outside world will, on reflection, be aware of the absurdity of what he has done while still believing in the ideas which, to some extent, had prompted him to behave in that way. It is a sense of personal absurdity, expressed through exaggeration and bathos, which runs throughout this poem. Surrey is aware of the foolishness of what he has done (lines 19-22, 25 and 44, can only be read humorously), yet still believes a denouncement of the god-forsaken city is justified.

7 *convert* change   8 *terror* fear of punishment   9-10 i.e., there is small hope of any improvement being brought about by words alone, as preachers know all too well.

33 *just shaped hire* justly ordained wages, just reward   50 *Endurèd* hardened   52 *weal* wellbeing.

29

14 *wealth* wellbeing, happiness   17 *right way* mouth, the direct passage to one's insides   20 *lines of true belief* passages in the scriptures on the impermanence of human life (Jones)? *assuage* fade away, grow less.   23 Youth is like a wild horse which requires the bridle and bit to restrain it. Now in old age he can be put out to grass.   24 He is *beaten* because he has never achieved happiness, and so, as a mere spectator, is better qualified to define it.   28 *to their time* at that time of their lives

30

A translation of Martial's *Vitam quae faciunt beatiorem*. It was particularly admired in the eighteenth century as showing that 'justness of thought, correctness of style, and purity of expression' for which Warton thought Surrey might 'justly be pronounced the first English classical poet'.

6 *charge* burden   8 *continuance* antiquity (in keeping with the *riches left* — inherited wealth — of line 3).

31

1 *wealth* good fortune   7 The Scottish expedition of 1542   12 *freeze* froze   13 He is now in France

32

19 *repair* 'confluence of people in or at a place' (OED)   27 *in ure* in use, in practice, in existence. In this instance *draweth in ure* simply means 'begins' or 'comes into being'.

33

This and the following poem are written as if by Surrey's wife. From autumn 1544 to spring 1546 Surrey spent much of his time in Boulogne, and is known to have had permission for his wife to join him refused on more than one occasion.

2 *step in your foot* join in the chorus   4 *skills* concerns

21 *the same* refers to the dreams in line 17   22 *T* is Surrey's
eldest son, Thomas, born in March 1536   27 *salueth* greets
(kisses in this case)   33 *unnethe* with difficulty; i.e., I can
hardly find any quiet place where I can unburden myself of
the unrest in my mind.

34 This line is corrupt. The manuscript has 'Some hidden
where, to steal the grief of my unquiet mind' which Tottel
renders as 'Some hidden place, wherein to slake the gnawing
of my mind', an obvious rewriting of an admittedly unsatisfac-
tory line. I have given a compromise reading which makes
sense without being too drastic.

34

This poem is known to have been set to music. It is the only
poem by Surrey in the Duke of Devonshire MS, where it is
written in the hand of Mary Shelton, Clere's mistress. It is
natural to assume that Surrey sent the poem to his wife, and
Mary Shelton was moved enough (with Clere also in France,
or dead) to make a copy of it.

8 If this brings to mind Wyatt's galley charged with forgetfulness
it is because both lines have the same source in Petrarch.
22 *in arms across* arms laid across each other   33 *drencheth*
drowns   40 *wealth* happiness.

35

Written in late 1545. Nott says this is in response to Geraldine's
marriage to Sir Anthony Browne, and although they had in
fact married three years earlier, the example of Surrey's own
marriage makes it a reasonable assumption that something
decisive happened in this year. It is difficult to imagine what
else the poem might be about, although interpretation remains
a problem even after making that assumption. The *guide* in
line 10, for example, is said by Nott to mean 'Reason' and by
Jones to mean 'Love'. A straightforward interpretation (the
poet attempts to escape from his obsession, but finally accepts
that he must remain in thrall, pleased with his pain) does not
seem at all satisfactory. If one sees it as meaning that Geraldine
(now really married) has told him to cease being 'her man',

upon which he leaves the country, thinks over his past life and is persuaded by somebody (or something) to mend his ways, the tension and bitterness of tone of the poem are accounted for (as also are the poems written to his wife during this period). But such an interpretation seems to be roundly contradicted by the obvious meaning of line 7.

10 *that plain* who directly   12 *Bullayn* Boulogne, where Surrey was governor. *Base* means occupying a low-lying position, so the lower part of the town is being referred to, which makes the hills seem odd unless this means the guide brought him through the hills to the low-lying town (with obvious allegorical overtones). 'Base' had the figurative meanings then which it has now, although the military 'base' meaning does not occur until the nineteenth century.

36

For an analysis of this poem see Fowler (*op.cit*. 31-7) who says, quite rightly, that the 'architectural impression that Surrey's best poetry can give remains largely unaccounted for'.

Clere died on 14 April 1545, some months after he had saved Surrey's life at the siege of Montreuil. He was Surrey's squire and constant companion (see note to poem 28). After the fall of Boulogne to the English on 11 September 1544 Surrey returned to Montreuil, having been promised reinforcements by the King (which arrived too late). News came that a large force of French were advancing to raise the siege, so Surrey launched an attack on September 19. With a small force he fought his way through to the Abbéville Gate, and held a position there against great odds until he was struck down. Clere cut his way through to his side, and was about to take over command when he received the wound which eventually led to his death. The English retired via Boulogne to Calais on September 28.

1 Clere was born at Ormesby in Norfolk. He was buried in the chapel of the Howards in Lambeth Parish Church.

2 i.e., although you were born of the house of De Cleremont (you are one of the Howards in death).

3 *Ormonde's race* means the Boleyns. Clere's mother was the daughter of Sir Edward Boleyn. His uncle, Sir Thomas Boleyn, Earl of Wiltshire and Ormonde, married Elizabeth Howard who gave birth to Anne Boleyn. Thus Anne Boleyn was cousin to both Clere and Surrey.

5 Mary Shelton was also cousin to Anne Boleyn, and Clere's mistress (see note to poem 34). *Chase* is the past tense of 'choose'.

6 During the expedition to Scotland in 1542 (see note to poem 24).

7 *Laundersey* is Landrecy. Surrey and Clere took part in the siege in October 1543. Bullen is Boulogne.

8 *Muttrell* is Montreuil. This and *Bullen* are old-soldier style.

14 *timely* early. However, 'timely' certainly had its modern meaning of 'opportune', as well as a sense of something being in time, of this earth, as opposed to being eternal. It is possible that all three meanings are involved here.

Last poems

Some of these biblical paraphrases, probably all of them in fact, were written during Surrey's final imprisonment from early December 1546 to 19 January 1547. As translations they are very free, based upon the Latin paraphrases of Joannes Campensis which were published in 1532. They are of no great literary interest to us since we have all grown up with the versions in the English Bible. Their main appeal is that they were written by a condemned man. The obvious autobiographical relevance of many of the passages is enough to make the rough, incomplete nature of the verses moving in a way that a more accomplished work might not have been.

37

4 i.e., did ill agree with a king. 11 *cure* care. Early in 1544 the Howards acquired St Leonard's Hill near Norwich. Surrey received the title from his father, changed the name to Mount Surrey, and the building of Surrey House was begun. According to Nott the house was in purely Grecian style, the first instance of neo-classical architecture in England. It was probably designed

by Italian architects who were then at the English court. Drayton refers to 'The sumptuous house...which, in the rebellion of Norfolk, under Kett, in King Edward the sixth time, was much defaced by that impure rabble.' There is no sign whatsoever of it today.

33 *abusèd fier* vainglory

64 All of Surrey's goods were to become the possessions of his enemies, as he would have been aware when he wrote this.

71 *search* seek   76 The line is metrically sound, *expense* being written as 'spense'. The final three lines are so free a translation they can be read as a personal statement.

38

The version of Campensis does not employ the well known parallelism of the Vulgate and our Bible ('A time to be born, and a time to die,' etc).

5-6 i.e., our chief pursuit is to root up with pain (strenuously) those grafted plants, of which we had hoped for fruit, just when they have come into blossom.   8 *shred* lop   9 i.e., each adverse threatening look of fortune makes us lament. 11 *guise* way of doing things.   13 i.e., which soon fade away and disappear.   15 *spare* use sparingly   20 *debate* strife (contrast line 28)   24 *fraughteth* fills   30 *search* seek out   39 *grisly* terrible   41-2 These lines are Surrey's addition, which suggests there is probably a personal relevance to the following lines about the throne.   43 *wandered* confused   45 *mood* mind   61 i.e., I shall bear with the load of a modest financial competence.   66 i.e., their goods got with strife.

39

This is the prologue to Psalm Eighty Eight. Mason suggests that the idea of a prologue was taken from Wyatt's example. Only one of these still exists ('Sometime the pride of my assured truth'), and it is addressed to 'Mine Earl', which is almost certainly Surrey.

5 Sir Anthony Denny, Member of the Privy Council, probably affixed the royal seal (Henry VIII being too ill) to Surrey's death

warrant.

40

Unlike Wyatt's Penitential Psalms (the conventional selection), the four psalms Surrey translated (three given here) were chosen for their relevance to his personal situation. In this psalm, for example, 'to please my foe' in line 9 is Surrey's interpolation, and the personal application of 13-14 and 19-31 is painfully obvious.

16 *bain* bath   *appair* harm   25 *endurèd* hardened

41

This is the prologue to Psalm Seventy Three.

11 Sir George Blage (or Blagge) had served under Surrey, and it is a reasonable assumption that he had an influence on Surrey's religious ideas. It was a quarrel with Blage which led to Surrey's being detained in the Lord Chancellor's house before being accused of treason and committed to the Tower; and it seems likely that this quarrel was deliberately caused by Blage (on the instigation of the Seymour faction) to get Surrey out of the way while the charge of treason was being prepared against him. Thus the prologue is a statement of reconciliation towards someone who had seriously wronged him, as was also the case with Denny in poem 39.

42

16 Their looks are lofty because they look up in supplication as they bow. *They* in this line are the people being bowed to. 27 The just are in terror of inquity   36 *dooms* judgments 37 *doubt* a difficult point of faith, not a form of disbelief. 43 i.e., hearts charged with care. Lines 43-8 are interpolated. Lines 49-50 are a free adaptation, and line 53 another interpolation. 60 *behight* promise

43

The incomplete, frustrated tone of the poem, and its being in rough hexameters, suggests a rough draft. The closing lines make no attempt at translation. It is what one might expect from a man who tried to escape from the Tower by climbing down his cell privy (it went directly into the Thames) and almost

101

succeeded.

3 *threap* press 4 *Buckled* prepared *scathe* harm
16 *marketstede* marketplace 18*reproach* disgrace
22 Although this is straightforward translation it probably refers to Sir Richard Southwell, his accuser and former friend.

25 This line is some evidence to support the theory that Surrey was a secret Protestant, and had taken into his confidence someone like Southwell or Blage (perhaps also referred to in line 22).

28 *ascends* is 'descends' in the original, and *him* in line 29 is 'them'. Alterations done to make sense. 29 *haulture* height

The translation ends with line 41, and from 42 onwards it becomes totally personal utterance. The friar has not been identified, although it must be someone who has assured Surrey that although his reputation may be harmed he will not be executed (45). It might be possible to put down the resigned tone of the preceding psalms and epilogues to a deception of that kind.

46 *patching* knavish. *wealth* wellbeing. The line is confused but must mean something like, 'I hate such hypocritical concern which gives a false sense of wellbeing'.

47 Padelford suggests *th'other Psalm* is in fact the verse which follows the one Surrey has left untranslated. Thus line 47 means, 'Cast thy burden upon the lord and he shall sustain thee,' and the verse in which he finds ease is, 'He shall never suffer the righteous to be moved.'

44

According to his son this was Surrey's last poem. Line 8 is missing.

13 Nott suggests *glass* is 'the reflective powers of the mind', and Jones appears to agree, although it does not seem to fit with the preceding line nor make sense of the one that follows. The final lines have defeated the commentators, not only because of their obscurity but also their tone, 'the harsh spirit ...incompatible with the resignation of one who has forgiven his enemies and is about to die' (Padelford). He wanted to date

it earlier, but it is hardly likely that Surrey's son was less well-informed about this than someone living four hundred years after the event. We must accept that a poem which begins in philosophical resignation (the 'sweet revenge' of the Christian who has nonplussed his enemies by mildly forgiving them) can also end with a bitterness which is not very surprising in such a situation. It is that contrast which makes the poem sound so true. The glass can then be accepted as a real mirror (or at least a mirror that is being imagined, one presenting actual images, rather than an abstraction like the mind), in which the condemned man sees his own face, the cureless wound which bleeds day and night being his mortality, the fact that his head is soon to be removed from his shoulders. If the wretch to whom this hap is granted is seen as Surrey himself, the final lines make some kind of sense; and if it is assumed the wretch is Southwell who would not fight with him, then it makes another. It is a fine ambiguity with which to end a life.